HOW I HELPED O.J. GET AWAY WITH MURDER

HOW I HELPED O.J. GET AWAY WITH MURDER

The Shocking Inside Story of Violence, Loyalty, Regret, and Remorse

MIKE GILBERT

Since 1947
REGNERY
PUBLISHING, INC.
An Eagle Publishing Company • Washington, DC

Cataloging-in-Publication data on file with the Library of Congress

ISBN 978-1-59698-551-3

Published in the United States by
Regnery Publishing, Inc.
One Massachusetts Avenue, NW
Washington, DC 20001
www.regnery.com

Manufactured in the United States of America
10 9 8 7 6 5 4 3 2 1

Books are available in quantity for promotional or premium use. Write to Director of Special Sales, Regnery Publishing, Inc., One Massachusetts Avenue NW, Washington, DC 20001, for information on discounts and terms or call (202) 216-0600.

To Debbie; my children,
Michael, David, Chrissy, Luke, and Lindsay;
and my granddaughter, Autumn

CONTENTS

PROLOGUE

"Sooner or later a man who wears two faces
forgets which one is real."

———

PRIMAL FEAR

I am not interested in anybody's forgiveness, but I do want to tell the real story. I want you to know what happened, why it happened, and *how* it happened. I want you to see us as real people, no matter how you may judge us by the end of this book.

Before O.J. Simpson killed Nicole Brown Simpson and Ron Goldman on the night of June 12, 1994, we were all people you might have liked. We worked hard, kept our business affairs straight, kept discretions (in personal matters), and watched each other's backs. There were four of us in the innermost O.J. circle: Skip Taft, Cathy Randa, Al Cowlings, and me—the lawyer, the personal assistant, the best friend, and the agent. During the trial we were inseparable, but the pain and stress dissolved our bonds and now there's just a resigned silence.

We weren't evil, stupid, or crazy, any of us. We knew O.J., we knew Nicole, we knew their dynamics, and we could see the evidence. But unlike you, we had a profound conflict: We loved him.

That does not change the bottom line.

1

He did it. Of that I am 100 percent certain. Maybe if we start there, you can relax a little, and not feel that anybody is trying to tell you two plus two does not equal four, that O.J. is innocent. Then maybe we can wind the film back to the beginning, and get it right this time.

It's been fourteen years since Nicole and Ron were murdered. For those of us on the inside, it's been like living on the deck of a sinking ship caught in a typhoon. The storm never lets up; it's never over. You think you can move on but you can't, because you're tied to this thing, and you can't get off. The reason nobody can get off is because the ghost of the story is still stalking us.

I believe O.J. came as close as he will ever come to publicly confessing last year, in his bizarre tell-all book *If I Did It*. But he couldn't go through with it. I see my book partly as the final chapter of his book—a way to finish what he started.

We *all* live in fear of the whole truth being told, because once it is, everybody's ghosts start to come out. Let me put it this way: We are all guilty of something. I'll start with myself—I am guilty of a whole lot.

Several months ago I had a dream in which my grandmother, who helped raise me, who loved me probably more than anybody ever has, placed her hand on my leg and said, "Michael, why are you crying?" I told her I was crying because I was unhappy. She said, "Michael, you are unhappy because you have gotten so far away from who you really are. I know who you really are. You need to return to being that boy that your grandfather and I knew and loved. Then you will be happy again."

I woke up sobbing, and cried for a very long time. That was the turning point—when I decided never to try to get back to the privileged life, the VIP treatment, or any of it. I decided to write this book and not worry about how I might come across. I decided to just tell the story as honestly as possible.

But you have to take the whole journey with me, not just tune in when the saga began for the rest of the country, on the morning of June 13, 1994. While the public was watching this unfold, we were actually living it. It's very easy to sit in front of your TV screen and thunder about right and wrong. It's another matter altogether when your friend, your client, your hero—or in my case, all three—is on trial for murder.

It wasn't until two years ago that I finally broke ties with O.J. altogether and told him never to call me again. I was through. I always said, and this shocks people, that I *could* forgive him the murders—I really could. Why? Because it was the worst night of his life. Because everything that night happened in the blink of an eye, and it's that blink that nobody can comprehend—not even O.J. How can we judge him, finally, if we don't know what happened in the fateful, dreadful blink of a moment? I tried not to, all these years. I do judge him *now,* however, based on everything that happened after that—the choices he has made since.

I wouldn't have thought this was true, but I have come to realize that the worst possible punishment for a man is not to be given a chance to atone for his sins.

Atonement for sin is partly a necessary act of catharsis—not just a merciful one—because otherwise the guilty are retried and rehanged every single day of their lives. But how could we forgive him for a crime he would not admit he committed? Instead we all became trapped in limbo, year in and year out, trying, and failing, to find a place on earth that was not tainted by it, where the truth didn't reach. In the void created by O.J.'s denial, an industry sprang up that would give us all a chance to find our right price, to choose how exactly we would compromise ourselves. We all had something to sell: some piece of the story, some piece of the lie, or some piece of the truth. Even O.J. became a participant in the end.

This entire saga is an extended act of role-playing, masking, posturing, and selling—selling trinkets of easy morality and quick salvation. What I hope is different about this book is that it contains firsthand experiences, and I have not altered them to make myself appear better than I was or am.

Speaking of selling, I should tell you straight off that my loyalty to O.J. was not purely emotional or personal—it was also professional. We continued doing the business we'd done before the murders—primarily the business of sports memorabilia, of signing items and selling them—all the way up until my final break with him, two years ago. We did this throughout his incarceration, up until the day of the verdict. This is how and why I wound up spending virtually every day with O.J., in jail, during the so-called "trial of the century."

I never lied to him, never told him I didn't think he did it. Over time, I became more and more disillusioned with him, and disgusted with myself, for all the lies I told for him, for everything I did to help him hide, move, and lie about his most valuable possessions, to hide his assets, to shelter his money. I found myself, pretty soon, outside of society, living in a twilight world, where truth was always negotiable, but where there was absolutely no peace of mind.

I once screamed at him: "You bastard, I *hope* you committed this crime because if you didn't, then all of our lives have been ruined for nothing!"

But I know he did it. He told me as much. But I'll return to that later.

You are wondering why I decided to write this book now, and if it is "all about cashing in."

Nothing is "all about" anything. I wasn't ready before. I was still working for O.J. and I was still an apologist for him, for myself, for all the positions we'd taken over the years, and for the decisions we'd made. And always in the back of my mind was that I didn't want to hurt the people this may hurt. For me, the decisions we made were rooted in my enslavement to O.J.'s charm and charisma, and in wanting to turn back, mediate, and negotiate with the elephant in the room: the murders. I was in denial and I was hooked in by choices I made from day one, the day of the blast, June 12.

Now I'm not.

The simple reality is that I have a story that I know you will want to hear and I am telling it. You are free to judge me however you wish.

What follows is my story—not as I dream it, or imagine it, or would like it to be—but as it actually was.

CHAPTER ONE

BE CAREFUL WHAT YOU WISH FOR

People always ask me what I miss the most about the golden years, as agent to one of the most iconic American athletes of all time. The five-star hotels? Flying first class? Being treated like a rock star wherever we went? The women?

All of that was intoxicating, and I enjoyed it more than I would like to admit. But what I miss the most dates back much earlier, to when I was a kid, in the eighth grade. That was just before the leap into real life, when my dream world still governed me. Like every other American kid at that age, I had a hero. Mine happened to be O.J. Simpson.

I watched his every game. I knew his every move. He was one of four people in the world I dreamed of one day meeting.

I can remember the smell of the black magic marker and the thrill I felt as I carefully drew the number "32" on the back of my white T-shirt from JC Penney, stretched against the kitchen table. Those of you who remember O.J. from before all this know that 32 was his number. I wore that T-shirt constantly in our local football games, yelling: "I'm O.J.

Simpson!" There was nobody on earth I admired more, or wanted to be more. We played football constantly in my neighborhood, Highland Drive, in Hollister, California, until long after dark most days, every weekend, every holiday, every chance we got. We drove our mothers crazy—we just wouldn't come home. In my case, my mother was actually my stepmother, but I think of her as my true mother.

My birth mother had us three kids when she was just a teenager, and simply couldn't cope. I was the first one she gave up—deposited on the stoop of my grandparents' house, and that was it. She kept my sisters a little while longer, but soon came and dropped them off too. I guess there's a lot I don't know. It's not a subject we like to discuss in my family. In any case, things stabilized after my mother left us. My father remarried, happily, and I became a fairly normal suburban kid.

My birth mother came to see me once in the eleventh grade when I was competing in a track meet for Hollister High. Somebody told her where I would be competing and she just showed up. My buddy Ray Sanchez said, "Hey Gilbert, there's a lady here looking for you who says she's your mother."

I said, "What does she look like?"

He said, "She kind of looks like you."

I looked over his shoulder, and saw her walking toward us. I stiffened, but I was glad to see her. We talked for a while. She took me to have a hamburger, then asked if she could drive me home, which I agreed to. I was quiet and a bit distant during the two-and-a-half-hour ride, which seemed like an eternity.

I didn't see her again for many years, until my grandfather's funeral, when my mother came over to give me a hug and to thank me for being there.

With biting sarcasm, I introduced my sisters, her daughters: "Surely you remember your daughter Sondra and your other daughter Debbie?"

She looked at me quizzically and said, "Of course I do."

I didn't let up. I said, "Do you even *remember* my birthday?"

"November 3," she said quietly.

"I didn't get a birthday card from you for my entire childhood, that's why I asked."

She fell silent. A few moments later, when my anger had passed, I started to regret what I had said, as I so often do. It's always like this: my anger flares and I say something cutting that I later regret. I wish I had just returned her simple gesture and kept my mouth shut.

I'm sure she did what she felt was best for my sisters and me. As an adult I've come to love her, and always will.

At a young age, one way I learned to conquer hardship, or at least escape it momentarily, was through sports. Once I discovered football, I was free. I loved everything about it: the excitement, the clarity, the suspense, the heroics, the perpetual chance at instant redemption. At center stage of my dream world was O.J. Simpson: flying, defying gravity. He was an *amazing* athlete. He had everything—speed, strength, grace, agility, the ability to turn on a dime, and an uncanny gift of acceleration. That was his most exceptional talent, I think, if I had to pick one—acceleration. He could go from standing still to top speed in four steps. He was just faster than everybody else on the field—they couldn't catch him. He did things on the field that I thought were physically impossible. He could run over you, he could run around you, he could run past you. His coach at USC said he was not only the greatest running back, but the best college football player he had ever seen. Had he not chosen football, O.J. could easily have been an Olympic track star—he was that fast. In fact, he and his teammates set the world record of 38.6 seconds for the 4 x 110 relay,[*] in Salt Lake City, Utah, in 1967.[**]

---

[*] Prior to 1980, running race distances were measured in yards. Today we know this race as the 4 x 100 after the switch to the metric system.

[**] This record still stands.

In January 1969, I took USC against Ohio State in the Rose Bowl for twenty-five cents, in a bet with my aunt. O.J. played brilliantly, but USC lost. I was crushed, and paid up the twenty-five cents. Stung, I promised my aunt, "One day I'm going to meet O.J. Simpson and get my twenty-five cents back."

Sometimes I wonder if God punished me for being so greedy about that quarter. But of course it wasn't the money—it was the emotion of losing. Twenty years later, when I was his agent and we were sitting on the patio by his pool, I told O.J. that story. I asked him for the quarter. O.J. did have a great sense of humor.

"*No*," he said. "Fuck you, Mike. I'm not giving you the money. Twenty-five cents? Fuck no. What the fuck do you want *me* to do? It wasn't *my* fault we lost. I had a great game and Ohio State had an unbelievable defense that year." O.J. ran 171 yards and scored a touchdown in that game.

In 1992, Skip Taft, O.J.'s business attorney and longtime friend, sent me a Christmas present. It was a check from O.J.'s bank account for twenty-five cents. It was itemized as: "Repayment of gambling loss on 1969 Rose Bowl."

I still have it.

I have been a sports marketing agent since the mid-1980s. I was never one of those agents who only watched the bottom line—I was always emotionally attached, more than the average agent. My childhood experiences made me form fierce attachments, and to fear abandonment above all else.

In my heart I identified with the fans; I *was* a fan. Even when I was moving among the elite, representing the athletes, I still felt my strongest affinity not with them but with the fans—who believed in something.

My career as an agent began accidentally, in my sophomore year in high school, in 1971. A bunch of us took a Chevy Suburban to the coliseum at Cal Berkeley to watch a Raiders-Rams pre-season game. We got there at halftime. After the game we went over to the locker rooms, hoping for autographs. I spotted one of the players—Ben Davidson—and I had an inspired idea.

"Uncle Ben!" I hollered, not quite loud enough for Ben Davidson to hear but just loud enough for the security guards to hear. The guards stepped away and I followed "Uncle Ben" into the locker room. I scored my first batch of football autographs that day.

Soon after that I started to understand and tap into the immense power that athletes have to do good. A friend of my brother's had been paralyzed from the waist down in a car accident. I called the Raiders office and made arrangements for a few players to come to a fund-raiser. They did. Very quickly and simply, we raised several thousand dollars for the family's medical costs. One of the players even visited him in the hospital, which gave him inspiration and made him extremely happy. In that moment, I saw both the power of celebrity and the power of athletes to give back. They are given so much because of a God-given ability—because they can run a little faster or jump a little higher than everybody else.

By the mid-1980s, I was continuing to do work with the Raiders players, and my reputation was growing. Before long, I signed my first superstar client—Marcus Allen.

O.J. and Marcus were uncannily similar in their career paths. Both were running backs, both were alums of USC, both won the Heisman in their senior year of college,* both were picked in the first round of the NFL draft, both were expected to make immediate impacts on their NFL teams, and both were later inducted into pro football's Hall of Fame. They also shared a tragic passion for the same woman: Nicole Brown Simpson. I'll return to that later.

---

* O.J. won the Heisman in 1968 and Marcus won in 1981.

I was Marcus Allen's marketing manager for about a decade in both Los Angeles and Kansas City. Marcus and I had a great personal and professional relationship; we were true friends and I thought the world of him. Before I started representing O.J., Marcus was my number-one star client. He gave me instant credibility in the industry. I handled public appearances, endorsements, and the merchandising of collegiate and NFL memorabilia for Marcus. This was when my own life began to change, in the late 1980s. Suddenly, I became a member of the elite. No more flying coach, no more Best Westerns, no more Denny's. Once I was representing Marcus, everything was five-star and first-class. I had money, I had influence, I had tickets to every game, backstage passes to concerts—whatever I wanted. Before long, I started to buy into that lifestyle, to believe that I "deserved" it, and to resent anything that fell short of my expectations. I realize, looking back, that this was also the time when all sense of innocence started to become eroded and lost.

Before long, part of my job for Marcus included creating smokescreens that allowed him to more easily cheat on his lovely wife, Kathryn. I would leave false messages on his answering machine at his request—asking him to appear in fictional contexts, to give him an alibi and cover for his trysts with other women.

I did it not only for him but for other athletes. I created alternate worlds for these guys to live in. My loyalty and honesty was to the athlete—not the wife. I didn't like that part of the job, but I did it, very well. It started to become depressing. I remember I used to tell people that we created illusions in the world of professional sports—that from the outside it's like *The Wizard of Oz* before Dorothy looks behind the curtain. I wanted people to think that my clients were witty, charming, intelligent, sensitive people, because that was the image that Nike or Reebok or American Express wanted to portray. That's what we do in sports marketing. We create illusions. I want little Jimmy to go to McDonald's, and on the way I want him to be drinking a Coke, bouncing a basketball with a Nike logo on it, while wearing a Nike jogging suit and sneakers, dreaming that he's his favorite ball player. In sports marketing, we create that dream—that illusion—and then sell it, sell it, sell it.

Pretty soon, I became an illusion myself. I started cheating on my own wife, even though I loved her more than anything in the world. I started thinking the only thing that mattered was not what I did, but whether I got caught doing it. I got caught up in the power trip. At the same time, I also started to like myself a little less every day. The less I liked myself, the more I had to prop up the image, to distract myself and others from what I had become. I started thinking I was better than and different from "ordinary" people. I moved among the gods, and although I wasn't one myself, I was still among the elite.

There were four people in the world I truly idolized and had wanted all my life to meet: Muhammad Ali, Clint Eastwood, Elvis Presley, and O.J. Simpson. To me they embodied perfection in the American male. Each, in his own way, was a hero, an icon, one who defied all expectations and rose above all the forces that threaten to drag us down in this life, make us ordinary, make us blend into the crowd and live and die without distinction. That frightened me more than anything—being ordinary. I respected only the *extra*ordinary.

I wound up meeting three of the four: Muhammad Ali, Clint Eastwood, and O.J. Meeting O.J., though, transcended my wildest dreams.

Here's how it all began: Marcus Allen had said on a few occasions, "I can set you up with O.J., you know." Marcus was good friends with O.J., and had been mentored and guided by him professionally. I told him I would be thrilled if he could make the introduction, but I didn't press the issue.

In 1989, late one night, I got a call. It was about 11:00 PM. I wondered: Who would call me at this hour? I answered the phone and a deep voice said, "Mike, this is O.J. Simpson."

I thought Marcus was playing a joke. "Fuck you, Marcus," I said.

"No, really," the voice said. "This is O.J. Simpson. Marcus suggested we might do some work together."

Then I heard Marcus laughing in the background and saying, "Mike, this is Marcus. I am here with O.J., but you are talking to him." I froze. I put on my best professional voice and said, "O.J., I apologize. I would be happy to discuss the possibility of representing you."

O.J. was very friendly and charming. He said he'd heard that I was one of the best, and he liked to hire only the best people.

We set a date and time. The plan was for me to meet O.J. and his assistant, Cathy Randa, at his office in Brentwood a week later. I was excited, starstruck, and a little nervous. As the time approached, Cathy Randa called me and said O.J. wanted me to meet him at his house instead, at Rockingham. I got directions.

"One thing, Mike," she said before we signed off. "He is very, *very* protective of his image. You have to be extremely careful. He can't stand letting people down, so you mustn't ever book him for anything if there is even the slightest chance he won't be able to make it. Everything has to be checked and double checked. His image is everything to him."

"Understood," I said.

Cathy had been with him forever, and was extremely devoted to him. Sometimes it seemed she was even more protective of his image than he was. In Cathy's eyes, the world revolved around protecting O.J.

When I arrived at Rockingham, I followed Cathy inside the gate, and we walked around to the back of the house. Within seconds, O.J. walked out, and introduced himself. We shook hands. He was warm, friendly, and hospitable—he offered me sandwiches and soda. The first thing he said when we sat down on the patio to talk was: "Okay, Mike Gilbert, what can we do to make some money? Whatever it is you do for Marcus, I want that. I don't have anybody who does that for me. Marcus speaks very highly of you."

I said, "It depends on how much time you have, O.J."

We discussed his schedule, and I remember he said, "One thing we have to make absolutely certain of is that I can attend every single appearance that you book for me. Sometimes fans have driven hours to be at an event—I've seen it—the disappointment on fans' faces when a celebrity doesn't show up. I don't ever want that to happen. So the first thing is, anything you book, we have to be totally sure I am going to be there. I don't want to disappoint my fans—ever."

After we had discussed business for about an hour and a half, we walked into the house. As soon as we walked in, I spotted the shrine. I think he saw the look on my face. He said, "Do you want to see my Heisman?"

Is the Pope Catholic?

We walked over, and looked at the glass-encased trophy. To me, it was like looking at the Holy Grail. Behind it on the wall was a game-worn jersey from O.J.'s last game at USC. He walked me over and showed me some of the other awards that he had received in the NFL, and told me a little bit about each one. Then we went into the pool room and he showed me some game balls and other mementos. I felt like a kid again—the same kid who yelled, "I'm O.J. Simpson!" It was like that kid had stepped into his own dream, twenty years in the future. O.J. seemed simply wonderful to me, beyond any expectation I could have possibly had. He was gracious, kind, warm, funny, and dignified. By the time I left that day, I felt like I had known him my entire life.

Over the next five years, which I call the "golden years," it was an absolute delight to be O.J. Simpson's marketing agent. Everything he touched turned to gold, everybody loved him, everybody wanted him. He was one of those athletes who represented something that was much more than the sum of his achievements. He was the god of flight. That's what people wanted from him. That's why all those people with the signs that said, "Go Juice!" lined the 405 as the white Bronco passed. O.J. remarked in his book that when he saw those people he thought, *"When did they have time to make those signs?"*

Being a fan myself, it didn't surprise me at all.

I saw it wherever we went. People wanted to touch him, shake his hand; they felt he had some kind of magic to impart. O.J. was larger than life, bigger than celebrity. He represented success, and *hope*. He embodied the American dream.

He had, after all, transcended some pretty tough odds. He'd grown up in a rough neighborhood, Potrero Hill in San Francisco, run in street gangs, had numerous run-ins with the police as a teen, and been raised by a single mother.

O.J. didn't talk about his father much, but when he did it was fairly affectionate. His father had done something unusual for that era—he came out as gay. He left the family, then stayed in the neighborhood, living as an openly gay man.

The most astonishing fact of O.J.'s childhood, to me anyway, is that he had rickets—a disease of malnutrition. His beloved mother, Eunice, blamed herself. It left him with skinny bowlegs, for which Eunice built homemade braces, successfully straightening them out. He had to walk around as a child, for hours every day, in iron braces—if that isn't symbolic, I don't know what is. O.J. came from an environment of very strong, churchgoing, and disciplinary women—his mother and his aunts. I think, if I may offer some dime-store psychology, that he both depended upon and raged against women's power. His greatest terror was to be abandoned—as I should know because I see this in myself as well, in the way I am with women.

Everybody *adored* Eunice. She was a wonderful woman and I remember her vividly—her warmth, charisma, humor, and earthiness.

It was Eunice who pushed O.J. out of the ghetto and into a life of sports. She talked the baseball coach at a local high school into giving him a tryout, but he lost his spot on the team when he failed to show up for a crucial practice. O.J.'s original dream was to be a major league catcher. In fact, one time when O.J. had gotten into trouble in the neighborhood, he came home and Willie Mays was sitting in his living room. Mays had heard about this incredibly gifted kid who was about to blow it. Mays had a heart-to-heart talk with O.J. and said, "You can really do things. You have *real* talent, but you have to stop messing around and being a thug, and concentrate on your abilities. It will not only take you a long way but you'll also be able to help your mother."

When O.J. was a kid, he once met his own idol—Jim Brown—widely considered the greatest running back, and by some estimates, the greatest football player of all time. The story goes that O.J. went up to Jim Brown and said, "Some day, I'm going to break all your records." Brown rudely dismissed him, saying something like, "Yeah, whatever, kid."

I have always believed that that was one of the reasons why O.J. was so intent upon never disappointing his fans, because he was so disappointed by Jim Brown's dismissive treatment of him.

Nonetheless, Jim Brown's number was 32, and that was always O.J.'s favorite number when he was a young athlete, until, that is, Willie Mays gave him this pep talk. He switched his number allegiance to 24—Mays's number.

When O.J. was a track runner, the number on his sweats was 24, and he wanted the number 24 on his football jersey at USC, but he was let down. He couldn't have it. With 24 out of the question, O.J. switched back to number 32 and kept that number throughout the rest of his career.*

O.J. always said that Willie Mays's visit was his turning point.

Soon he discovered the sport for which he was fated.

---

* O.J. did wear the number 36 for a very short period of time when he was a rookie at Buffalo.

Sheila Weller, in *Raging Heart*, quoted O.J.'s description of his discovery of his football talent. O.J. was standing near a vacant lot, watching some other young people shooting off guns.

"I had to get through that lot. . . . I stood there and figured I was gonna run this way, then that way, then the other way—to get my ass through those bullets. I saw the *course*. I saw myself doing it *before* it happened. That was it, man: visualization."

O.J. Simpson literally came running into professional football through a blaze of bullets. That's how he learned how to run like that— that's how he became "O.J." This talent for flight was the premise of his Hertz commercials—O.J. dashing, hurtling, and even flying through an airport, with that cute little old lady—remember her?—yelling "Go, O.J., *go!*"

They even made a commercial in the early 1990s for an 800 collect calling company featuring Eunice hurtling over her rose bushes to get to a phone when O.J. called. It was very funny—we loved it. Eunice got $50,000 to shoot the commercial and O.J. got $100,000 just to agree not to make a competing commercial that year. That was probably the easiest contract I ever negotiated for him—he was thrilled. He got paid a hundred grand to not do something he wasn't going to do anyway.

In his youth, O.J. was not a particularly tough guy, but he was on the cusp of delinquency and trouble. It has always seemed to me that he was in equal parts disciplined and indulged. He had been relentlessly teased about his father's homosexuality, as well as about the size of his large head, his crooked legs, and the thing he hated most—his name. Orenthal was a name given to him by one of his aunts, who mistook it for the name of a famous French actor. He turned it into "O.J." (his middle name is James) and never looked back.

Even beyond his athletic persona, I think O.J. was feeding us fantasies at a deeply subconscious level, like the dream of a post-racial America, where everything is forgiven and redeemed. Or rather, we were conjuring this ourselves, through him.

O.J. himself didn't dwell on racism much, it's true. Or rather, not before the murders, he didn't. He loved my Muhammad Ali story more than anything and made me tell it all the time. The story was from the first time I met Ali in the late 1980s on a trip to San Jose with a bunch of my athletes. I was virtually the only white man in the room. I held out my hand and said, "Muhammad Ali."

He made a fist, leaned toward me, and said, "Did you just call me a niggah?"

The whole room went quiet.

Sensing a twinkle in his eye, I gambled. "Not yet I didn't."

He grinned. I realized he was playing with me. "Come on, champ," I said.

"Chump?" he said, taking a step back. "First you call me a niggah and then you call me a chump?"

He put me in a headlock and started hitting me on the top of the head, real soft. "You're uglier than Joe Frazier, stupider than George Foreman," he said over and over.

As he let me out of the headlock, acting like we were being pulled apart, I said, "Come on, champ, you don't want any of this."

"I want *all of it*," he roared. He walked across the room to the door, turned back and pointed at me, he then made a fist and bit his lip, as if to say, *I'm coming for you one day.*

It was all for fun, just a really magical moment.

Minutes after he left the room, his agent came over to me and said, "Do you know why he did that?"

"No, why? Because he hates white people?" I said jokingly.

"Because for the rest of your life, you're going to remember the time you met Muhammad Ali. You'll tell this story a thousand times." He was right, I probably have. Muhammad Ali and I spoke about it again five years later when I ran into him at a hotel after I attended the Super Bowl with O.J. and Nicole.

O.J. *loved* that story. We'd be in a room full of black athletes and he'd yell, "Hey, Mike Gilbert, don't you have a story to tell about the time you called Muhammad Ali a nigger?"

Everything in our world was lighthearted, jovial, fast-paced.

We spent a lot of time at Rockingham. It was the central hub of activity. Instead of meeting at O.J.'s office or Skip's office, we'd just meet there. I remember once back in 1992, Skip and his wife were over at the house, and the three of us were in O.J.'s kitchen talking and hanging out. O.J. was racing around packing, getting ready to leave for Barcelona where he was going to cover the 1992 Olympics for NBC. He was always a whirlwind before he was leaving for a trip, and this time he was going to be away for several weeks.

Skip had opened the fridge and taken out some little jars of caviar, which we were enjoying on some crackers. O.J. came flying into the kitchen and stopped dead in his tracks.

"What are you guys eating?" he said, with alarm in his voice. "Are you eating my caviar?"

Skip looked at the label on one of the jars. "Apparently we are, O.J." he said cheerfully. "It's delicious."

"That stuff is like sixty dollars a jar, and you guys are just standing there wolfing it down?!"

Skip calmly smiled at him and said, "Sixty dollars a jar…really? Well, good thing there's one jar left. I think we'll take that one with us to the movies tonight."

We were all laughing and O.J. kept the joke going all night until he left. The best part was that Skip and his wife actually did finish that last jar of caviar at the movies that night.

We used to have a lot of fun together.

We weren't standing around trying to be perfect citizens. Now, it's as though everything any of us ever said or did—especially O.J.—is a prelude to the murders. But none of us could have predicted the murders or dreamed them in our worst nightmares.

The year 1994 was promising to be one of our best. We were on top of the world. In the previous year, I had secured many new and lucrative contracts for both O.J. and Marcus. We were attending World Series games, NBA playoff games, Super Bowls, parties everywhere. O.J. was a broadcaster for NBC sports, was on the board of directors for Victorinox Swiss Army, was doing countless gigs as a representative of Hertz rental cars, and had started filming the final *Naked Gun* movie. He even did the coin toss at the 1993 Super Bowl in Pasadena.

O.J. shot three *Naked Gun* films, and I was on the set for the third one in 1993. I remember this filming, about a year before the murders, as one of the happiest times we had. We were like a big, happy family—we had such a blast. O.J. and Nicole were attempting their reconciliation and I remember her calling him numerous times on the set.

I remember one of those calls quite vividly. I was sitting with O.J. in his trailer during a break in the shooting of *Naked Gun 33 ⅓*, in 1993, when Nicole called. I gathered from O.J.'s end of the conversation that Nicole was very sad and depressed about getting old, about being thirty-four, and thinking the best years of her life were behind her. O.J. was very warm, sympathetic, and empathic. I was surprised by how sweet and kind he was on the phone toward her. "Nicole, listen," he said. "You are a thirty-four-year-old woman, and you're beautiful. You're gorgeous. You're worried about crow's-feet? So what? You're thirty-four, not twenty-four, and you can't pretend you are. You can't go back to being twenty-four again. Be who you are."

He kept saying the same encouraging things to her over and over, and finally when he hung up, I said, "Damn. Does she know she's your *ex*-wife?"

O.J. said, "Mike, how could I not care when she is sad and depressed? She is the mother of my kids. I love Nicole, but I'm not in love with her. Wouldn't you talk to your ex-wife if she were upset?"

"No, I don't think so," I said.

Ironically, not long after that, I got a similar call from my ex-wife, Geralyn. She had recently divorced, and though we hadn't really talked about it before, on this occasion she opened up. She was very depressed, and admitted that she was having difficulty with the whole process. I consoled her as best I could, and I remember saying, "Geralyn, I love you. I will always love you. One of the greatest mistakes of my life was ruining our marriage."

We had a wonderful heartfelt conversation and I think we both felt a lot better. Upon hanging up the phone, I remembered what O.J. had said. I got it. I knew what he meant. Once you've been married to someone, you always care about that person. The bond of marriage never breaks…it just changes.

I think about how Nicole must have felt at that time. Her concern about aging suggests that she felt she was losing her looks, the only power she felt she had, while O.J.'s power at this time was only growing. Everyone wanted to be around O.J., even presidents.

O.J. was a member of the Riviera Country Club, a very elite, expensive country club with a championship golf course. Just weeks before the murders, in the spring of 1994, one of the Riviera Hotel executives came over to O.J. after a golf game and asked if he wanted to play golf with the president the next day.

O.J., in genuine confusion, replied, "The president of what?"

"The president of the United States."

"Oh! *That* president. Sure."

So the next day, sure enough, O.J. and President Bill Clinton played golf. I was disgusted when O.J. told me this, because I despise the Clintons. O.J. and I argued about it a bit. He said, "Mike, if you met him you'd like him."

"No, I wouldn't."

With characteristic diplomacy and social ambition, O.J. said, "Mike, no matter who is in the White House, it's always good if they're your friend."

I remember him telling me that he'd made a putt that impressed Clinton, and that O.J. had cracked, "That's why they call me the Juice." Then Clinton made a putt and said, "That's why they call me the Prez."

O.J. told me that Clinton had waxed enthusiastic about Anna Nicole Smith, who had a part in one of the *Naked Gun* movies. He had drawled, "I saw her and I said, 'There goes the White House.'" O.J. was much less enthusiastic about Anna Nicole.

Also around this time, spring of 1994, I began negotiations to have Ronald Reagan, who was a big sports fan, sign 1,000 baseballs. His representatives were interested in this in order to raise funds for the Reagan Library, and also said that President Reagan wanted to meet O.J. We worked very hard on scheduling a lunch with the three of us, but O.J.'s *Naked Gun* shooting schedule made it impossible.

I was very disappointed. Ronald Reagan was my favorite president. He sent me a personalized autographed photo, but I deeply regret letting that lunch slip away.

President Reagan's representatives later offered to have former president George Bush sign the baseballs instead, and as an extra bonus, they said one of his sons, George W. Bush, then the governor of Texas, could co-sign. But I only wanted Ronald Reagan. Like so many strange deals that have crossed my path, I said, "Great idea; let's forget it."

My judgment wasn't always perfect, to say the least. Wouldn't it be great now to have one of those Bush baseballs?

CHAPTER TWO

JUNE 12, 1994: THE END OF THE WORLD AS WE KNEW IT

It was shaping up to be a perfect weekend. My two star clients, O.J. and Marcus, were both taking off on trips that weekend, all their contracts were in good shape, and I was finally taking a vacation.

I am an experienced rock climber, and my favorite place to climb is Yosemite National Park. I go there to find solace and peace, but it's also something a little more complicated. My sister Sondra says I used to climb very deftly, in order not to fall, but that now—after all that has happened—I seem not to be so careful. I think she's right. I used to climb to get to the top, but in recent years that hasn't always been the case. Sometimes I climb not to. Often I have thought, one single ill-placed foot and I could fall into a place where nobody has a name, or a face, or a history—where nobody ever heard of O.J. Simpson.

It was my weekend with my kids from my first marriage. My son David said he wanted to come and climb with me at Yosemite. My daughter Chrissy decided to stay in Hanford, and my eldest son, Michael, was working and couldn't make the trip. The weather was balmy and warm that time of summer, early June. Our lives were pretty great. Money was good, business was good, and everybody was healthy. The only thing that was clouding my mind at all was the problem with O.J.

I had spoken to O.J. the day before we left for Yosemite, June 10. His voice and intonation sounded dark, strange, and depressed. He sounded like a slowed-down audiotape version of himself. Everything about him was different—everything.

It wasn't the first, but the second, time I had encountered this weirdly altered O.J. on the phone. The first time was late May or early June, when I called him from the Hyatt Hotel in Kansas City to ask why he had not signed and returned a $100,000 endorsement contract. That, first of all, was totally unlike him. In business, he was 100 percent dependable. Now he wouldn't answer his phone and ignored a barrage of pleas from me to sign the contract and fax it back before we lost the deal. When I finally got him on the phone, I was met with that deep, distant-sounding voice. It was as though his soul had left his body. He sounded empty, depressed.

I was very worried and even unsure if this voice on the phone really belonged to O.J.

I asked him:

"O.J., what year did you win the Heisman?"

He answered groggily, "1968."

"And what year did you run 2,003 yards?"

He said every number, slowly and individually, *nineteen . . . seventy . . . three.*

I hung up and immediately called Skip Taft, O.J.'s business attorney, mentor, and guiding light for two decades.

"Skip," I said, "what is wrong with O.J.?"

Skip sighed, in that gentle, fatherly manner he had when things got rough, and I remember verbatim what he said: "Mike, Nicole has O.J. so fucked up, he doesn't know whether he's coming or going. He doesn't know what's up or down." That was the only time I ever heard Skip curse.

After a pause, I said, "Okay," but I wasn't satisfied with that explanation, because with Nicole and O.J., that was just business as usual. They were *always* driving each other crazy.

It was only later during the criminal trial that I learned that O.J. had been placed on a heavy dose of an anti-depressant drug—something O.J. later said was supposed to make him feel better but that only made him worse. I believe it was Prozac. That was why he sounded like that. Knowing O.J., if the doctor told him to take two a day he would take four.

Skip told me to fax the contract to him, and said he would take it over to O.J.'s house at Rockingham, have him sign it, and fax it back to me. That was how we resolved it.

On June 12, David and I climbed the Royal Arches—a fairly short climb by Yosemite standards. The next day, June 13, we woke early and hiked to the top of Yosemite falls, looking out over Lost Arrow Spire. That was my Moby Dick—the one climb I had never done. I had been scheduled to do it ten years previously, but my then wife, Geralyn, told me she had a dream that if I climbed it I would die, so I never did. On this crisp, perfectly still morning, David said, "Dad, you should do it."

"Okay," I said right away. I was ready. I was exhilarated, but that feeling would not last long. After the ascent, we hiked down to the bottom of Yosemite Falls to use the payphone and call home to tell them what our plans were. I got the answering machine at the house and started leaving a message for my wife, Debbie. She picked up the phone and cut me off.

"Mike," she said, "Nicole's been murdered and O.J. is in handcuffs. You need to get to Rockingham."

After a brief silence, I said, "So he finally did it."

Debbie shut off the answering machine.

"*What did you say? Why would you say that?*"

Everything was already filmy, nauseating, unreal, like after a car crash.

"I don't know," I said. "I don't know why I said that."

I tried to steady my mind. I remembered that O.J. was scheduled to fly to Chicago the night before, and I clung to that. I immediately started looking for reasons to believe he didn't do it. David was in shock, pale and quiet.

"David, we've got to go."

We packed up our stuff and raced out of Yosemite Valley. I must have been driving 100 mph on the straightaway stretches. We had no radio or phone reception for about an hour until we got to the town of Oakhurst. I turned on the radio. The story was everywhere. I started making calls on my cell phone. I called all of O.J.'s numbers, not expecting to reach him but wanting to get a message through to him. I called *everybody*. And everybody called me.

When I finally walked in the front door of my home in Hanford, Debbie, Chrissy, and my other kids, Luke and Lindsay, were all in front of the TV. The story was on every single channel. There was O.J. with his hands cuffed behind his back. I was totally lost, slightly out of my own body. The phone rang off the hook. Friends, business associates, clients—everybody was calling. I finally got to the point where I just answered the phone by saying, "I can't talk," click. "I can't talk," click. "I can't talk," click.

The inner circle, the outer circle, and every possible layer of any O.J. circle that ever existed were calling my house. People we were doing business with, with whom we had signed various sorts of contracts, were wondering what to expect and whether they would get their money back.

"I don't know what to tell you," I said. "The guy's wife's been murdered and he's in handcuffs. We have to wait and see. I don't know any more than you do."

O.J. was released after being questioned. The inner circle immediately became a crisis-control unit. We tried to act normal in an extremely abnormal situation. All I remember of our conversations back then is that they had this strange, slow-motion, nightmare quality. Every word you're hearing or speaking is something you never thought you'd hear or say.

One conversation that still stands out in my memory fourteen years later was the one I had with Marcus Allen. I reached him that first day, June 13. Everything about the conversation was puzzling and peculiar. It didn't make sense then, though it does now.

I called Marcus's house and got his sister-in-law, Debbie, on the phone. She said Marcus and his wife, Kathryn, were in the Cayman Islands, which I knew. They had flown out late the night before.

"Does Marcus know what's going on?" I asked.

"Yes."

"Tell him I need him to call me."

Marcus called moments later.

"You know what's going on?" I asked him.

"Yes," he said. He asked me how I was.

"Blown away," I said. "I can't believe Nicole is dead. When are you coming back?"

I expected him to say, "Immediately."

Instead he said, "Mike, I'm not coming back."

"What? *Why*?" I asked, absolutely blindsided. "You're going to come back for the funeral, aren't you?"

Again he said flatly, "No."

I couldn't comprehend anything anymore. Marcus and Kathryn had been married at O.J.'s house. He had been friends with O.J. since he was in college.

"Mike, it's going to be a media circus," he explained. "It's going to be crazy. You shouldn't go either. There is no need."

I remember saying to myself, well, if one of their closest friends isn't going to the funeral, I certainly don't have to go. So I let myself off the hook, too. To this day, I regret it. I never liked Nicole much and she never liked me, or, more correctly, we never really bonded much, but I should have gone to her funeral.

That was one of my first mistakes. I think the deeper reason I wanted an excuse not to go was that I was beginning to really believe that O.J. did it, and I didn't know how I would face him or what I would say.

I got off the phone with Marcus and resumed calling O.J.'s house. I finally got an answer—it was Gigi, the housekeeper.

Gigi sounded very nervous. I said to her, "Tell O.J. if there is anything at all that I can do, I'm here. And tell him . . . I'm sorry."

The phone rang ceaselessly over the next few days. This was when the whirlwind started to become a typhoon. I was trying to stay under it all, and yet at the same time, on top of it all. I didn't want to go to L.A. I just waited until there was a need.

On June 17, the day O.J. was to voluntarily turn himself in to the authorities, I called the house again and told Gigi to tell O.J. that I was coming to Los Angeles. I got in my car and started driving. As I got about 100 miles north of L.A., it came on the news that O.J. was wanted by the police and that they were actively searching for him. I thought Jesus, *did he kill himself?* Is he that spun? I called every number I ever had for him—cell, car, everything. Then, suddenly, O.J.'s friend Bob Kardashian came on the radio and started reading O.J.'s suicide note. I could not believe this *was actually happening.* I started praying: please don't let him throw his life away. We can get through this. What time did his flight leave again? He couldn't have done this. This will all be straightened out. Please don't let him commit suicide.

I ended up going to the Hyatt, went to my room, and called O.J.'s cell phone. "O.J., it's Mike. I'm at the Hyatt hotel. If you need anything, *anything at all*, call me. Whatever you need, I'm here." I left the phone number to the hotel and my room number.

I turned on the TV, and within seconds they broke away from the NBA championship game and showed grainy footage of a car chase. The newscaster said, "The vehicle you are seeing is believed to contain O.J. Simpson on the 91 freeway, in flight from police cars who are pursuing him."

My hotel phone rang. It was the hotel operator. "Mr. Gilbert, someone called for you. They were inquiring about your last name, but they have a package for you from UPS."

That sounded implausible. Nobody knew where I was, and I most definitely wasn't expecting any package. I told her that if they called back, to put the call through. Seconds later the phone rang again and a voice said, "Mike? You don't know me. I live near O.J. in Brentwood. O.J. got his cell phone from the shop I work in, and, uh, I got my phone there too. Sometimes we get our messages crossed and stuff."

It was obviously either the cops or the tabloids picking up every message that went to O.J.'s cell. The guy got right down to it. "Do you expect O.J. to call you back? Who is A.C.? What did you mean 'If you need *anything*?'"

"Yeah, right," I said. "I doubt anybody who lives in Brentwood works in a cell phone store. How stupid do you think I am? Who *are* you?" I never got an answer.

The TV was showing the white Bronco on the 405 now. I hung up, ran out of my room, and jumped into my car. I knew O.J. was going home, to Rockingham. As soon as I got onto Sepulveda heading toward the 405, I looked toward the southeast and saw a swarm of helicopters; I knew that was where O.J. was. By the time I merged onto the 405, I was about a mile behind him. I exited at Sunset Boulevard and headed toward Rockingham.

As I got close to the house, the streets were blocked by police barricades. People from the media were everywhere. I parked the car and started walking toward Rockingham. I got stopped at a barricade. The cops told me O.J. had not yet surrendered, and that nobody was coming in or out until he had. I showed them every piece of ID I had.

"*I'm his manager,*" I pleaded. "Let me talk to him. I need to get in there. Look," I said, showing the cop my cell phone, which listed all of O.J.'s numbers. I scrolled to his home number, and dialed. A police officer answered, identified himself, and I hung up. I told the cop, "That should confirm that I am who I say I am."

I started to panic: I overheard reporters saying there were sharpshooters in the trees because O.J. had a gun. The word was they were going to shoot him. I wheeled around to the nearest cop and got right up in his face.

"*If you fuckers kill him there will be hell to pay. Do you understand? You think we had riots in L.A. before? Let me talk to him!*" Suddenly O.J. was a man with a gun surrounded by SWAT teams. I was in a cold sweat, walking in circles, mumbling and praying that he would surrender. That was all I wanted at that point. "*Surrender*, Juicer, goddammit," I muttered.

I don't know if twenty minutes passed, or three hours, but finally, I heard what I wanted to hear—O.J. was in police custody. I felt a radiating wave of relief through my whole body. The police car with O.J. handcuffed in the back seat drove right past me, less than ten feet away. I could see O.J. in there, dully staring straight ahead. He looked like a wax figure of himself. The reporters started to walk back toward the main entrance road, like a herd just fed and moving on. I went to my car, feeling absolutely physically and emotionally drained. I sat in the driver's seat and wept. At least he was in custody, I told myself, happy that he was still alive.

CHAPTER THREE

DANCE MACABRE

We'd all been watching tentatively as Nicole and O.J. tried to reconcile their marriage during the year before the murders. They were fully divorced, but felt they might be able to put things back together. The plan was to date for one year, from Mother's Day 1993 to Mother's Day 1994, then make a decision. It was toward the end of that year that things grew ominous. It was obvious to most of us that it wasn't working out, that they were repeating the same cycle that drove them apart in the first place.

O.J. and I were sitting in his office on San Vicente Boulevard and he asked me very sincerely, "Mike, I'm thinking about getting back together with Nicole. What do you think?"

"I don't think you should do it. You've got to give it time. Neither one of you has really changed yet. It won't work. You can never go back again to the way it was."

O.J. listened, then said, "Okay, man. Thanks."

I remember Cathy Randa was dead set against it as well. Really, nobody thought it was a good idea, except for O.J. and Nicole.

Things got worse and worse, and reached an all-time low point start-ing on Mother's Day, 1994. Nicole had even given back, in a move that was not like the old Nicole, O.J.'s Mother's Day gift and birthday gift to her of a diamond bracelet and diamond earrings (which he then gave to his girl-friend). That was when things really spun out.

Throughout this "reconciliation" year, O.J. and Nicole were in that very brittle phase couples can get into when they have broken their bond, but not accepted the fact. They were trying to have it both ways—being together and not being together. In the weeks leading up to the murders, things got steadily more complicated and volatile. Nicole had rather actively been pursuing O.J. for some time, calling him constantly, and springing surprise visits on him at out-of-town events, which was not good because he often had other women around. It fell upon me and Cathy Randa to clear the runways in time for Nicole's surprise arrivals.

O.J. liked it when Nicole was chasing him, though he sometimes felt oppressed by it. Sometimes I remember Nicole would call, O.J. would put her on hold, and just leave her there, then not answer when she called back. Nicole had not reacted well to being put out of the castle—Rockingham—where she was queen. In her condo, lavish though it was, she lost status, she was just another rich California divorcée—no longer the wife of an icon. She was pushing hard to move back into Rockingham and really make it work again. O.J. basically shunned her. The simple truth is, he was enjoying all his other women, and he also liked keeping Nicole dangling, so long as the roles remained with O.J. in control and Nicole in pursuit.

Nicole had a real temper. She was not a good drunk, and O.J. was no better. When the two of them would start arguing it was not fun to be around. We all dreaded it.

I was with O.J. on October 25, 1993, the day of the now-infamous 911 call that Nicole made, pleading for cops to come save her from O.J., who had virtually broken down the door. I remember it for a couple of reasons: number one, it was my wedding anniversary; number two, I have never, ever experienced O.J. in a mood that foul—not even when he was in jail.

O.J. was filming scenes in the *Naked Gun 33 ⅓* movie in the Shrine Auditorium in L.A. and I'd driven down so he could sign Heisman footballs and work on some business affairs in between scenes. I had my son Luke with me. Normally O.J. was incredibly charming, charismatic, high energy, but on this occasion he was just in a horrible, *very* foul mood. I finally said, "O.J., what's the matter?"

He said: "It's just more Nicole bullshit."

"Like what?" I asked.

"Oh, it's just more of her fucking bullshit. I'm just fucking tired of it."

He always said, afterwards, that his mood that day was perfectly normal, but that is a total lie. Within a few days he was telling all our mutual friends that everything was "great" that day. As usual, he blamed everything on Nicole to anybody who would listen.

I remember looking at my watch and saying, "It's my anniversary, O.J. If I don't get to the restaurant in time for dinner, I'll have another ex-wife."

I remember he said, "Well, that's the *last* motherfucking thing you want is another ex-wife."

He wound up going over to Nicole's house on Gretna Green that evening—the night of the 911 call. Something obviously set him off, beyond the—by then—six-month-old news that he'd found Nicole giving oral sex to a bartender named Keith Zlomsowitch in her living room while the kids were asleep upstairs. At the time, O.J. told me he had rung the doorbell and left, just to let Nicole and Zlomsowitch know someone had been there.

I don't know what it was that enraged him that day, or that night, October 25, 1993. I talked to him the next day. He told me what had happened—that Nicole had "wound up" calling 911—and immediately started justifying it. He said they were just "talking," and that he was urging her to be careful how, when, and with whom she "fooled around." He felt that the bartender was beneath her, and he didn't want people like him around the kids.

Nicole had retorted, "O.J., I don't want you stopping by here uninvited. You have no reason to come here uninvited, ever." She was basically telling him he was a stalker.

I remember O.J. trying to sell me on a convoluted scenario involving his foot being in the door when she was trying to close it. "I didn't break the door down. Mike, she was trying to close the door *on my foot*." I remember in that moment that I didn't believe him. I didn't believe a word he was saying and he was starting to exhaust me from the energy it took just to play along. It was starting to become a very simple pattern: Everybody else is wrong, always. O.J. is never wrong. Never.[*]

The 911 story wound up in the *National Enquirer*, and according to Faye Resnick, Nicole's new friend, O.J. called Nicole when she was on her way to the airport with Faye to go on a trip, and said, "Get a copy of the *National Enquirer* at the airport." In it was an account of not only the 911 call, but also of O.J. and Nicole's attempted marital reconciliation. It was so detailed, O.J. was certain it must have been leaked by somebody in Nicole's inner circle.

O.J. did love Nicole very deeply, but he was also very angry at her for the way he felt she treated him. He felt that without him she would have been just another uneducated girl, a waitress, and that because of him, she lived a millionaire's life. He felt she was disrespectful, despite the fact that everything she had was because of him. He felt that she let her "trashy" friends use her and spend his money.

The avalanche started with a few pebbles: Everything that could go wrong in the weeks and days leading up to the murders, did go wrong. Everything.

---

[*] Listen to the audio of Nicole's 911 call at: http://www.courttv.com/video/archive/.

Emotionally, what was going on with O.J. was that Nicole had finally rejected him in a very, for him, humiliating way. She had communicated: "I don't need you. Get lost." This happened as a result of his rejection of *her*, when, in the months and weeks before her death, she tried to persuade him to let her move back into Rockingham. He rebuffed her, and finally she said, well the hell with it then. That was when she really started showing O.J. in no uncertain terms that she did not want or need anything from him. She repeatedly told him this. But the simple truth remained that she did need him, if for nothing else, for financial support.

Yet, in the last weeks of her life, she had done a complete about-face, and stopped doing the same dance steps that the two of them were accustomed to. She just pushed him straight away from her, as though she were truly finished with him. Faye Resnick encouraged her in this direction. Faye was telling her, "You don't need him," and encouraging Nicole to come out and party and develop a new life with new friends, which she did.

O.J. and Nicole had been fighting for seventeen years at that point. In her book *Raging Heart*, Sheila Weller recounts that on Nicole's nineteenth birthday she was having breakfast with her family when they heard two cars pull into the driveway. They went outside and found a Ferrari with a huge bow on it. Nicole said, "Dad, I have been seeing somebody. I think you have heard of him. He's a football player. His name is O.J. Simpson." Weller quotes the family describing Lou Brown's reaction to the news that Nicole was dating O.J. "I think my father's reaction," Denise said, "was, 'Well, if it's gonna be a black guy, I'm glad it's someone who's not a bum.'" The reason O.J. had given her the car was to apologize for the very first black eye he'd given her, which she had covered with makeup, so nobody noticed it.

They had divorced in 1992, but as various books—including one of O.J.'s—have described, they still had a stormy, addictive, passionate relationship that kept them bound to one another, through countless brawls, splits, reconciliations, and even serious beatings. They knew how to push each other's buttons. O.J. would kick down a door, bash Nicole's car, or "get into a tussle" with her, as he put it—that is, hit her.

I am as guilty as everyone else of looking the other way when it was obvious that O.J. was abusing Nicole.

In Nicole's diary, she describes returning from a Disney on Ice event when she was pregnant with Justin in 1988. We see a very different O.J. from the one who "loved Nicole" and who allegedly was himself a victim of domestic abuse. Nicole wrote:

> We went to the show and when we got back he was still gone. When he and A.C. [O.J.'s friend Al Cowlings] got back A.C. seemed strange, like he was waiting for something to happen, that they might have discussed. He kissed Mama, Mini, but not me, which is weird for A.C. O.J. was drunk. Mama and Mini felt something too. They started to leave and O.J. started saying things about not being invited. No room for him. I said that he made excuses all week. Well, he followed Mini and Mama out the door rattling 100 miles per hour about what a liar I am. He never stopped. He followed Sydney and I around the house. "Please, don't yell and scream in front of Sydney." So A.C. grabbed her. And I tried to get him away from her so she wouldn't have to hear it. He never let up. "You're a fat pig. You're disgusting." (I'm two months pregnant.) "You're a slob. I want you out of my fucking house." Then I took Sydney to bed, tried to anyway. And he proceeded to cut me down with A.C. in the entry downstairs. I tried to tape the conversation but the recorder didn't work. He was saying all those things again so that I could hear every word as he was telling A.C. "My wife's a fat ass, a liar. I stopped fucking other girls and now I jack off, the fat ass."

He locked me out of our room and I buzzed him. "Get out of my fucking house you fat ass liar." He opened the door and started off on me again. "I want you to have an abortion with the baby." So I packed a few things together. He locked the door again. I buzzed. "Do I really have to go tonight. Sydney is sleeping. It's late."

"Let me tell you how serious I am. I have a gun in my hand right now. Get the fuck out of here." I got real scared and grabbed Sydney and the cats and a bag for her and a bottle and a pair of sweats from the laundry room for me and got the heck out of the house.

When this was read to A.C. when he was being deposed in O.J.'s 1996/97 civil trial, he claimed to have no memory of the event. It must have been devastating for A.C. to hear Nicole's words. Her torture and conflict are reflected so clearly in everything she wrote—the combination of submission and strength, of trying to get close and trying to get through to O.J., to make him hear her.

Maybe Al was just suppressing the memory. We all did a lot of suppressing. I have much more sympathy for Nicole now, especially now that I, in some sense, have managed to break the spell of O.J.'s charisma. If you had asked me whether Nicole was a battered wife prior to the murders, I might have said no.

Nicole made at least three calls to the police—in 1985, 1989, and 1993. Imagine how many times she must have almost called, or wanted to call, or started to call. O.J. powerfully spun these incidents—insisting they were minor scrapes, the kind all couples have. Although we didn't completely believe him, the incidents and the underlying implications, in each case, were soon forgotten. Just like Nicole's friends and family, we were blinded by the fact that she seemed so in love with O.J. and was always back in his arms no matter what. I kept thinking: How bad can it possibly be if she keeps coming back to him? Nicole and I weren't very close. I didn't hear her side of the story. I always heard O.J.'s side, which was that everything happened because Nicole overreacted, or was violent, or drunk, and he was *always* the victim.

O.J. was a domineering authoritarian, a controlling patriarch, a sounding board, friend, and quasi-ex-husband. Nicole both wanted to be free of O.J. and begged him to put her back in her cage. Neither of them could make up their minds.

Each of them had their allies and confidants, and I was of course strictly on O.J.'s "side." Whenever he asked me if I thought he should get back together with Nicole, I always said, "No way." I didn't think it would ever be different, and I was exhausted myself, seeing O.J. always so stressed out, angry, and unpredictable. Every day it was something else. If Nicole pissed him off, he took it out on us.

They had other lovers and separate lives, and they continued to wear down their already frayed bond with transgressions and confessions. I am not going to attempt to dethread this dynamic, because I think O.J. has given his side of the story and, through her friends, we have Nicole's side too.

There is no disagreement on any side about the simple, essential facts: they had a very powerful love and bond, and they were obsessed with each other.

With each new lover, they were just feeding their addiction to the one thing that was the core of their lives—the other. It is true that Nicole worked very hard at persuading O.J. to take her back and let her and the kids move back into Rockingham the year leading up to her death, and it is true that O.J. rebuffed her. He enjoyed being free to date other women, and he also enjoyed, to an extent, watching Nicole crawl back to him. When she stopped chasing him, he absolutely hated it.

Deep down, Nicole loved and adored O.J. no matter what was going on between them, and he absolutely felt the same about her. But at the very end, he started to become so frigid toward her that it slowly generated a new feeling in Nicole: contempt. And this threw O.J. off completely—the concept of her totally and utterly cutting him off.

O.J. felt that Nicole needed him more than he needed her, so when she put up a new and very icy front, when he could see the resolve in her, it triggered a flood of new emotions for O.J. that he couldn't deal with. Now *he* was the one being left. We could see in his demeanor that this time was different.

She was hanging out with her new gang of girlfriends, with Faye Resnick at the center. Faye would field calls from the two of them, often at the same time, clicking back and forth. My impression was that Faye influenced Nicole to make a real, final, and unequivocal break from O.J. When she finally did, just days before her murder, it was because she herself had begun to truly dislike and disdain him.

Why? Because he crossed a new line of cruelty. Nicole was falsely claiming a tax break by telling the IRS she lived at Rockingham. O.J. had one of his lawyers send her a letter threatening to turn her in to the IRS. *That* was when Nicole truly, once and for all, decided she was "done" with O.J.

Nicole wrote her in her diary:

> O.J. came to pick up kids at 8:30 PM. This is June 3, 1994. They wanted to stay home because I let them organize sleepovers at last minute. Thought daddy wasn't coming. Told O.J. I'd drop them off first thing in the morning. He said okay. Then "you hung up on me last night. You're gonna pay for this bitch. You're holding money from the IRS. You're going to jail you fucking cunt. You think you can do any fricking thing you want. You've got it coming.

I've already talked to my lawyers about this bitch. They'll get you for tax evasion bitch. I'll see to it. You're not gonna have a fucking dime," et cetera. This was all being said as Sydney's girlfriend Allegra was being dropped off. They may have already walked into the house. I'm not sure if they had heard all or any of it. I just turned around and walked away.

The perfect storm was brewing, and it didn't take long to hit.

According to Faye, Nicole, with Faye's counseling, had planned very carefully how she would shun O.J. at Sydney's middle-school dance recital that afternoon. It was partly in retaliation for his cruelty to her and his increasing disregard for the kids, and partly because he had failed to show up for Sydney's first communion reception. Also, Nicole was *furious* about the IRS letter.

So Nicole, and by extension her family, cut O.J. off cold, even refusing to let him sit near them at the recital. He had to sit behind them. Then, when the family went out to dinner at the restaurant Mezzaluna afterward, O.J. was explicitly not invited.

If you knew how enmeshed all these people were, you'd understand how extreme that was. Something was clearly marked on June 12: Nicole was finished with O.J. and showing him that she "didn't need" him. Kato Kaelin later testified that O.J. came home from the recital really angry about it. It had started a fire in his mind. He always ranted about how his money paid for everything Nicole had, so this was a sore spot. He railed that she could only pretend to be independent of him. She had a generous divorce settlement: nearly half a million dollars in a lump sum and $10,000 a month in child support. O.J. felt like he owned her, *and* her family.

And there she was treating him with a level of distance and disdain he'd never seen before. He just went into a very bad tailspin. The dance was over.

I believe there was one more fatal element to that night: Nicole had been having a relationship with Marcus Allen. Marcus Allen, O.J.'s good friend and protégé. Marcus Allen, my friend and client. I did not know this at the time. I know this now because Marcus himself told me so, not long after the murders. So did O.J.

I'll describe those conversations in more detail later.

According to Faye Resnick, despite O.J.'s threat that he would kill Nicole if she started seeing Marcus again, she did. Her friends told her this was like signing her own death warrant. They were horrified to find Marcus's car at her house right out in the open, when O.J. could drive past. They were very afraid of this affair—of her seeming nonchalance about it—and believed it could get her killed. Marcus, after all, was one of O.J.'s best friends. O.J. never expressed rage toward Marcus directly—that part is true—but he was definitely enraged about it.

Faye Resnick said that when she spoke to Nicole on June 12, she was on "cloud nine" because of Marcus. She reported that Nicole was in love with Marcus, and that she'd said he was the second love of her life after O.J. Faye concluded that Nicole "had seen Marcus that day, [June 12] or she was going to see him. I knew how she got when she was going to be with him."

I have always thought that, even though Marcus flew to the Cayman Islands late on the night of June 12 to join his wife, he was with Nicole either that day or earlier that night, and O.J. saw them together.

CHAPTER FOUR

BLOOD BROTHERS

O.J. was incarcerated on June 17, on the evening of the Bronco "chase." In the days that followed, I mostly recall a dense blizzard of phone calls, and the way we defined our loyalty to O.J. Who would crack first? What constituted normal behavior in this extremely abnormal situation? What about ethical behavior? In the beginning, we focused on getting organized.

I remember the first time I spoke to Skip Taft about what was happening. A few days after the murders, Skip and I had lunch at our usual place, the Daily Grill on San Vicente Boulevard, and ordered the same lunch we always did, Cobb salad and a bowl of Manhattan clam chowder. Skip had been O.J.'s business attorney for more than two decades at that time, and I had been O.J.'s marketing agent for about four years. Seen from the outside, this was a normal lunch between two business associates. But between us was something so alien, it was hard for us to find words at all. We discussed the discussable first: how to handle O.J.'s corporate sponsors and business partners, who had been calling nonstop since O.J.'s arrest. We talked about how to offer reimbursements and how we could, with dignity and decency, resolve O.J.'s many outstanding contracts.

Toward the end of the meeting, I finally asked him, "Skip, what do you think is going on? What do you think happened?"

He looked at me with a slight sadness in his eyes and said, "Mike, I have known O.J. for over twenty years and I have never known him to lie to me. He said he didn't do it. Until he says otherwise, I will believe him."

I respected that, and I still do. In fact, when I look back on what Skip said that day, I feel nostalgia for that moment, when Skip believed in O.J.'s innocence, and that meant we could too, because Skip was so much like a father figure to us.

I can say flat out that Skip Taft is the most upright, ethical, and dignified man I have ever known. He was like a living incarnation of Atticus Finch, or the grandfather everybody wishes they had had.

Looking back on it now, I think Skip was talking about the concept of a person being innocent until proven guilty. He wasn't talking about evidence. He was talking about a *spirit* of goodwill. He wanted with all his heart to think that O.J. did not do this. Skip truly loved O.J. He simply had no guile, intolerance, venom, or any similar qualities. Skip became like a lighthouse for me, a way for me to always find the shore.

The next hurdle we all faced was visiting O.J. in jail, seeing him actually behind bars, our roles now totally shattered and recast. O.J. was always the seat of power and we always followed and served him. Now he was in jail, accused of double murder.

Several of O.J.'s friends, about fifteen to twenty people, visited him on the first day we were permitted access, about a week after he was incarcerated. Marcus and Kathryn went there, and Cathy Randa of course, and Ron Shipp, a friend of O.J.'s who wound up testifying for the prosecution.

Jail is jail—a very hopeless, depressing, claustrophobic environment. To get to O.J., we had to go through metal detectors, followed by two metal doors. The first one bolts behind you before the second door opens. We sat in a waiting room, and then went in, singly or in pairs, like Marcus and Kathryn. The visiting room was the size of a walk-in closet. We sat behind a desk, separated from O.J. by a glass partition.

I walked in to see him, and—imagine this—he was shackled, sitting behind this partition. The chains around his waist rattled when he moved. You could tell he was self-conscious about it. That alone just about broke my heart. He was wearing a blue jumpsuit. I remember how defeated he looked. That aura that he always had was gone. He didn't have the charisma anymore. He wasn't "O.J." He was . . . mortal.

The partition was about three feet high, and on later visits I was allowed to pass things over to him, but I couldn't touch him. I couldn't hug him or shake his hand. Instead, just like they do in countless movies, we put our hands up to either side of the glass.

I was afraid to make eye contact with him because I was scared of what I would see. So I looked down at his hands, where I saw a big, swollen gash on the middle finger of his left hand.

It was macabre, but I remember looking at that knuckle and wondering when exactly the knife had cut it. Was it when he was killing Nicole? Was it when he was killing Ron? I don't know, and I doubt he does. I do know, however, that he will carry that scar on his knuckle to his grave.

I finally looked him in the eyes, but he couldn't look back at mine. I kept searching for words. I couldn't bring myself to say, "O.J., we know you didn't do it." It wouldn't have been true. I looked at his hands, his eyes . . . and I could just see it. I remember thinking, "What *happened* to you? How could you go so far and not catch yourself? How could you throw it all away?" I kept waiting for him to say, "Mike, I didn't do this." But he didn't.

It was so uncomfortable that our twenty-minute visit seemed like an eternity.

I finally said, "O.J.... is there anything at all that I can do?"

"Yeah," he said darkly. "Get me the fuck out of here."

In our circle you could already sense the power of the unspoken ocean beneath us. The thing we all seemed to fear most in those early days was being seen as having betrayed O.J. There were no good options: we were damned if we did and damned if we didn't. We could choose between being damned by the public, the inner circle, our families, our wives, or finally, ourselves. It came down to picking one course—there was no way *not* to be damned.

The first friend who did "betray" O.J. was Ron Shipp. He was the very first Judas.

Shipp started out adamantly supportive of O.J. He came over to me in the hallway that first visiting day, and I remember exactly what he said: "I hope they get the guys who did this because O.J. doesn't deserve to be in a place like this."

I nodded. "I hope so too."

I know what you're thinking: "What about you, Mike Gilbert? By writing this book, have you not also become a Judas?"

Yes, I have.

I have countless stories of how and when people started "betraying" O.J. I was always very scornful of such people, but now I am one of them. And now, finally, I understand why they did it. It is something you are driven to, in an attempt to reconcile your actions with your conscience—to return to planet Earth from an exile so terrible you can't imagine it unless you've been through it.

Two people were killed that night, but there were many other casualties. For many of us, everything that had once been alive and good started to die and rot. The dream we had been living died—our sense of self-worth, dignity, and community. It was like the sun was snuffed out. We all drifted farther and farther from normal society and from one another. Being labeled as a band of complicit knife-sharpeners, we absorbed tremendous, relentless hostility that continues to this day.

O.J. was the super-pariah, but we were all made into smaller pariahs. My wife, Debbie, had to absorb repeated death threats against me. There were times when she pressed the play button on our home answering machine to hear not only curses and abuse, but even the promise that we would one day return home to find our own children dead and bloodied on the front porch like Ron and Nicole.

By protecting O.J., we were protecting ourselves. Or rather, we were *trying* to protect ourselves—our names, reputations, our standing in the community, and, in a current that ran contrary to all that, our sense of loyalty to O.J. Like I said, in a situation like this, there are no good options; there are only bad ones, and even worse ones.

Another casualty was my marriage. The stress of the trial dissolved our bond of marriage. I'm incredibly proud of Debbie though. She was lost in a dark place for a long time. But she found her way back into the light. We have thus far failed to rebuild our marriage, but I will always love her.

Guilt and innocence always seemed so clear to me before I landed in the middle of this. I'm ashamed of much of what I did, but not all of it. Looking back, I realize a lot of our misdeeds grew out of a conviction that we were behaving *as good friends should.* But we didn't realize how we were losing sight of reality—losing our souls—little by little. Before long we started to lie to ourselves and believe every word. Each step took us deeper into a dark forest from which we hoped to escape.

But we never really made it back.

Until that terrible night in June 1994 we had been living the American dream. It never occurred to us that it could all be lost in a matter of seconds, in an incomprehensible bloodbath.

As for Ron Shipp, what I recall was that he switched sides after a writer who was working on a book about the Brown family coaxed him into saying things that hurt O.J.'s case. O.J. pieced together the information in the book and figured the "leak" could only have been Shipp. We started to shun him. That was when, I think, the prosecution got to Shipp. For him, it was like choosing between freezing water and sharks.

Shipp testified that O.J. told him he had a dream in which he killed Nicole and wanted to know if that would cause him to fail a polygraph test. I thought Shipp was lying. But over time, as the evidence unfolded, I came to believe Shipp's testimony. It was unconscionable for our side to vilify him as we did—calling him an alcoholic and so forth. He's another person I would like to apologize to personally. On his Web site, he described his ordeal in terms with which I could empathize. It made me realize that for those of us who were on that road together, each path taken led to the same result, the same desolation. Shipp wrote:

> My grueling two days on the witness stand, which consisted of a barrage of attacks on my character by O.J.'s "Dream Team" of attorneys, was the worst experience of my life. I believed nothing in life could ever make me feel that bad again. I was wrong! In the years that followed, living in the Trial of the Century aftermath was an absolute nightmare! Not even my Police Academy training, or my decade and a half as a Los Angeles Police Officer, could have prepared me for the tumultuous ride after the trial.
>
> In the years that ensued, lies were told and stories were spread about me by people I knew and even from some I didn't know. Devastatingly enough, the crushing blow was when two of my closest friends contributed to the fabrications. Feeling betrayed, I remember praying, "God, I didn't ask for this notoriety, and only you know why I was placed in this 'lying's' den." As I grew increasingly disenchanted

with some of my close friends, the "system," and just life in general, I knew I was in need of some good therapy if I was to mentally and emotionally survive this ordeal. I was afraid to seek professional help, because even some psychotherapists were selling their stories to publishers or the tabloids. My generally fun-loving disposition turned inward, gray, and depressed. The game face I wore during the trial finally shattered, rendering me exhausted and depleted.

Despite the risk of betraying my friends, I finally decided that going to my grave without putting this down on paper was no longer an option. In a catastrophic situation like the one we faced, a group starts out huddled together, protecting itself from the onslaught. But eventually the pressures become so monumental that people start to crack, the community is destroyed, and it's every man for himself.

CHAPTER FIVE

THE SHOW MUST GO ON

"The people like to be humbugged."

———

—P.T. Barnum

Before I saw O.J. in jail that first time, I was actually summoned to see him but could not get in. That was the day I realized that O.J. had a survival mechanism that bordered on shocking. He kept his eye on the ball, no matter what.

O.J. had been in jail for about four days when I received a phone call from Cathy Randa. I was driving back from the San Diego area, from a meeting with the Ted Williams card company, when I got the call. Cathy said, "Mike, O.J. wants to meet with you. Do you want to go see him?"

"Absolutely. Of course I do." I wasn't sure what was going on, but I had a hunch.

Cathy explained how to get to the jail, where to park, how to get past the media hordes outside the jail, and whom to look for when I got there.

"Nicole will meet you there," she said.

"*Nicole*?"

"Yes, Nicole Pulvers—from the attorney's office."

"Oh. Okay."

Nicole Pulvers was a young attorney just out of law school who was assigned to stay with O.J. at all times and to communicate his needs to the rest of us. As long as Nicole was in the attorney room, O.J. could be there too. If there were no attorney there, he had to stay in his cell. O.J. later told me that he found the silence in his jail cell deafening. He hated being alone in there.

I drove to the Los Angeles County Jail and walked through the sea of reporters into the jailhouse. Nicole found me in the lobby, and I started going through the security checks. When they ran my name though the computer, they said I was not allowed to go in because "material witnesses" had not yet been approved. Nicole went in to explain the situation to O.J. as I waited in the lobby.

A short while later, Nicole came back: "O.J. is livid. Furious."

"Why?"

"He says that they are messing with him by not letting you in, because you are on the material witness list and you should be approved by now. He feels they're just playing games with him, trying to break him down."

She handed me a note. "This is from O.J."

I recognized that it wasn't his handwriting on the gray-tinted note paper.

It read: "Mike, I need you now more than ever. Imagine: *O.J. Simpson, Los Angeles County Jail.* My autograph is worth more money than anybody alive."

I looked at Nicole.

"Is this what he wanted you to give me?"

"Yes. He dictated it and made sure I wrote it down, word for word."

"Why didn't he write it himself?"

"He can't be given a pen."

I stared at the note in shock. My God, I thought, here his ex-wife has been dead less than a week and he's already thinking about business and making money. I was floored. But I regained my composure and started thinking the way my client wanted me to: about business.

O.J. wanted to begin signing autographs again, despite the fact that he was in jail—or rather, precisely *because* he was in jail. He wanted us to kick into high gear, and start making money through signature sales. He was saying: "Mike, get to work."

Cathy and I were divided on the issue. Cathy felt strongly that there should be no business while O.J. was in jail. I was ready to do whatever O.J. wanted. We turned to Skip, who considered the matter carefully, as he did all complications in our increasingly bizarre lives. Pretty soon he made a decision. "Look, we need to generate money," he said. Sensing the distress in Cathy, he assured her, "We are going to do this in good taste."

By mid-July we decided—since O.J. had always sold signatures in the past, and since these were strictly sports signatures—that we would indeed go back into production and have O.J. sign autographs from jail. Skip's directive to do this in a dignified and legal way required a bit of fancy footwork and research. To our knowledge, a prisoner had never signed autographs from jail before. Skip consulted the famous civil liberties lawyer Alan Dershowitz about O.J.'s First Amendment rights, and we justified the endeavor to ourselves by asserting that O.J. had not yet been convicted of any crime. We eventually received permission from the courts and the sheriff's department to proceed with the signing of sports memorabilia.

We started with cards—the easiest. We had a contract to sign 5,000 cards for a company called Signature Rookies, featuring an action shot of O.J. in his Buffalo Bills uniform. The authorities prohibited him from adding "Los Angeles County Jail" to his signature, but we got around that by having O.J. date his signatures, which showed he'd signed the cards while incarcerated. A signed O.J. Simpson card before the murders had a market value of about $25. These went for $250 each.

The whole process moved slowly at first. I'd give ten cards at a time, along with the pen, to a lieutenant, who'd pass them to a sergeant, who'd give them to a guard. The guard would take O.J. out of his cell, hand him the pen, O.J. would sign the cards, and then hand over the cards and the pen. They would put him back in his cell and send the signed cards back through the chain of command to the lobby, where I would retrieve them. Then we'd start the whole process over again. We did this for about ten hours every day in the beginning.

After a few days, they told us we could send in a hundred cards at a time. But a funny thing started to happen: I never got a hundred cards back. I got ninety-two or ninety-four—never a hundred. I counted and recounted, and it happened every time.

I decided to talk to O.J. about this. It was not easy to talk to O.J. on the phone. O.J. had to call Cathy Randa collect from the jail payphone, and she had to put him on hold and patch me through from the lobby, even though he was less than two hundred feet from me. Finally, he came on the line.

"O.J.," I said, "are you by chance keeping any of the cards?"

He erupted. "Why the *fuck* would I keep any of these cards, Mike?"

I had my reasons for asking; I thought maybe he was using them to barter with the guards. But he said no, so I explained what was going on with the missing cards. We didn't know what to do, so once more we turned to Skip.

"Skip," I said, "the guards are lifting some of these cards from us."

Skip mulled it over. It could be that the sheriff was purposefully having this done so that we'd raise the issue. Then he could say, "I'm not having my guards accused of theft. Bullshit. *Shut it down*." A complaint from us would've given them a pretext to end our whole operation, and in fact, every day we expected them to do so.

Skip finally said, "Mike, let it go. This is just the cost of doing business."

So we continued. We got back ninety-two or ninety-four, out of every one hundred cards, and we never said a word. O.J. signed a total of about 5,000 cards that first round.

At this point the sheriff's department allowed me to sit with O.J. in the attorney's room, as long as Nicole Pulvers was there. That was when we knew we were really open for business. We turned to photographs next: glossies of O.J. playing at USC or in the NFL. He probably signed around 10,000 of those, maybe more. Then we became more ambitious: we had him sign footballs, jerseys, posters, lithographs, serigraphs, movie scripts—you name it, he signed it. He signed a couple hundred Leroy Neiman serigraphs from jail. He signed collectible calling cards. Johnnie Cochran signed 1,000 trial photographs for me one day in a small room behind Judge Ito's chamber and another 2,000 at his office on Wilshire Boulevard.

We had to be very creative about transporting the goods into the jail. For example, we couldn't bring in football helmets due to their bulk, and also because the facemask set off the metal detectors. So we ordered helmet decals and had him autograph those. Normally a helmet is signed right on the helmet, so these decal-signed helmets are more valuable among memorabilia collectors who know that O.J. signed them in jail.

Footballs are also pretty bulky, but we solved that problem, too. Since footballs are made of four leather or vinyl panels, we had a company deliver the individual panels to us. We brought in briefcases filled with 150 panels at a time. As for the jerseys, we brought just the numbers, the 3 and the 2, and he signed one or the other. Later, we had them sewn onto the jerseys.

We had him signing autographs for the entire duration of his incarceration, clear up to the day of the verdict. Business was booming. In fact, business had never been so good. O.J.'s statement that his autograph was worth more than any man's alive proved to be correct. But we were walking a very fine line. O.J. was very strict—we all were—about not crossing that line, not signing anything at all that was connected to the trial. But people kept trying, and it was tempting. We had one guy offer us $250,000 to autograph 1,000 photographs of O.J. that were taken when he made his plea to the court: "I am absolutely, positively, one hundred percent *not guilty*." O.J. declined the offer. "That was spoken from my heart, and isn't for sale," he said.

That was back when he still cared about, and believed he could restore, his almighty image.

It's hard to calculate exactly how much we made during O.J.'s incarceration, but it was probably in excess of $3 million. I don't think anybody really knows. It all went toward funding O.J.'s astronomical legal defense costs.

While O.J. was in jail, we were approached by an investor named Lenward Holness, who wanted to manufacture sculptures of O.J. and sell them. Holness pulled up to the jail in a Rolls Royce in a pinstriped zoot suit. He looked to me like a cartoon character who was up to no good. But he had money.

He paid us something like $75,000 cash for the rights to make limitededition bronze figurine sculptures of O.J. in his Buffalo Bills uniform. His plan to sell these statues was to get an 800 number and place ads in sports memorabilia magazines and newspapers. A classic American entrepreneur, you might say.

Holness hired a sculptor, and we supplied him with countless photos of O.J., mostly game shots. The sculptor created a prototype that was about eighteen inches tall, and probably weighed about twenty pounds. When it got to the final stages, I had to bring it to O.J. so he could critique it and make "corrections." I had to lug that damn thing in and out of the jail, praying each time that O.J. would be satisfied with it. It was heavy. O.J. would examine it and give me a list of corrections: "the lips are all wrong, the face is too long, the body is too short." Once he said, "My legs don't look muscular enough," and I looked right at him, with my most sardonic face, and said, "O.J., you had fucking *rickets*. That's what your legs *look* like, give me a break!"

They finally finished the thing. I have no idea whether they ever sold any of them, but I seem to recall they were charging something like $5,000 a piece, so I rather doubt it. That is one piece of O.J. memorabilia I never want to see again.

You can't imagine the offers that were constantly coming in, every one stranger than the next. No matter how much people were outraged by O.J., I can tell you there was no shortage of entrepreneurial types knocking at our doors, wanting to cash in. I think this is the thing that makes America itself: we are a people of noble values, but slightly ahead of them runs a quality that mitigates them, takes the edge off: our greed.

I said that O.J. never allowed the trial itself, or the murders, to be exploited. There were two exceptions. The first was a photo of O.J. and Johnnie Cochran at the trial, signed by both of them. The second, believe it or not, was a birthday card.

A company paid us $50,000 to record O.J.'s voice for an electronic greeting card. We had to tape-record O.J. saying: "Hey, this is O.J. Simpson, I hear it's your birthday. Happy Birthday to you." I don't really recall, but I think the front of the card said something like, "I Did It," then you opened it and it said inside: "I remembered your birthday." I brought him the script in jail, then went to my phone so he could call me collect and we could record the message for the card. We did several takes, like you always do when you record voiceovers. It was hard to get good sound quality and I finally realized what the problem was. "O.J.," I said, "Sit *still*. I can hear your chains rattling in the background."

The card was perhaps in poor taste, but it wasn't *our* idea. I have to admit, I would like to get my hands on one of those. It was a great idea, in its own way.

CHAPTER SIX

O.J. IN JAIL

O.J. remained behind bars for about sixteen months, from June 1994 to October 1995, while his trial played out.

O.J. absolutely hated being in jail—he hated everything about it. He was used to having his food cooked to perfection and staying at the finest hotels in the world, so how would you expect him to feel about it? Once, when I was sitting with him in jail, I remembered having a meal with him at his house in Rockingham, and recalled that he refused to use paper napkins—he insisted on cloth at every meal.

Seeing O.J. in jail tore me apart. It may disgust you to hear me express sympathy for him. But this doesn't mean I didn't also sympathize with the murder victims, the kids, and the victims' families. The two didn't cancel each other out. The world isn't that simple, try as we might to make it so. It's true that O.J. and I were friends, while Nicole and I were not. But that's the thing—O.J. *was* my friend, and long before that he was my idol. I loved him. And I felt sorry for him.

In jail, at least he was protected from all the hate and he knew what to expect from one minute to the next. Unlike a segment of the public, the jail guards treated him well. When he got out, he never knew where or when the next person would hiss "murderer," or walk out of a restaurant at the mere sight of him, or spit on the ground after he passed by.

In jail, things were predictable and ordered. Because he was incarcerated, the people around him didn't feel the need to lash out with their own personal punishments. They left him alone. They accorded him his dignity.

He had a few perks, but was by no means given special treatment. He was allowed to use an exercise bike on the roof, and that was important to him—he liked to keep fit. He lost a lot of weight in jail, mostly because he often skipped meals in order to stay in the attorney room.

O.J. was in the same high-profile jail wing as Lyle and Erik Menendez, the brothers who were being tried, and would later be convicted, for the shotgun murders of their parents in their Beverly Hills home. They sometimes passed us in the corridors or sat in the adjoining visiting room. They saw O.J. signing autographs, and they had their attorney ask me whether I could help them do the same. I politely declined. I remember O.J.'s indignation: "All they ever did was kill their parents. Why would anybody want *their* autograph?"

Once O.J. leaned toward me and whispered after the Menendez brothers had just walked past, "Mike, you want to hear a really strange coincidence? A weird story?"

"Sure."

"Well, Mr. Menendez, their father, was an executive at Hertz, and I met them and signed a football for each of them. It was when they were kids, so it was sometime in the 1980s. And now here we all are, in jail together, on the same floor. Talk about a small world."

There was an additional element of macabre coincidence: O.J. told me that one of Nicole's baby showers, for Justin I think, had been held at the house where the Menendez parents were later murdered. The Menendez family leased the house from O.J.'s friend Mark Slotkin.

There were several famous killers in O.J.'s wing. In addition to the Menendez brothers, there was Joe Hunt, for example, of Billionaire Boys Club fame. Once, when Hunt was passing by, O.J. fell silent and watched him. Then he leaned over to me and said, "There's a cold-blooded killer right there. Look at that guy. He has absolutely no emotions."

Sometimes when we were sitting there in jail, with O.J. chained to his chair, under the fluorescent lights, with the musty airless smell, the hopeless environment, and depressed out of our minds, he would start to tell stories, out of the blue.

Game stories.

He was a phenomenal storyteller, and over the years, a few stories became such classics that we'd sometimes ask him to repeat them to us, as if he were a musician and we wanted him to play our favorite songs over and over. I would look over at Skip and he would have tears in his eyes and he would say, "I could hear that story a hundred times, O.J.; I still tear up." When O.J. would tell a story we would be transported right through the walls of the jail and onto the field, with the crowds roaring and the wind on our faces, like we were *there*. For those minutes, however long it took O.J. to tell the stories, we were not in jail, we were somewhere else; it sometimes felt like we were inside the huddle.

He liked to tell one story about a crucial Bills-Jets game at Shea Stadium in 1973, the year he became the first running back in history to rush for more than 2,000 yards in a single season.* The Bills had to win the game or else their season was over. The Bills had the ball, the clock was winding down, and the coach was shuttling wide receivers in and out of the huddle to bring plays to the quarterback. This was before they communicated through mics and headsets.

---

*He still holds the record for a fourteen-game season.

The coach sent a player called Crackback Jones to give the quarterback the play. His nickname stemmed from the crackback block—an illegal block that can severely injure the opposing player. Crackback had a stuttering problem, and he stuttered the worst when he was under a lot of stress. His only way around his stutter was to sing whatever it was he was trying to say.

Standing in the huddle, with the clock ticking, Crackback was stressing out. He was stuttering, "Buh buh buh buh." Everybody leaned in closer. "Buh buh buh buh buh..." Finally, somebody yelled at him, "Just fucking *sing* it!"

So Crackback, at the top of his lungs, started singing the play. They broke the huddle, and the guys were still laughing and grinning as they went to the line of scrimmage. The Jets defense looked at them as if to say, "Are you guys crazy? The clock is winding down, you've got to score, and you're *laughing*?"

To O.J., the point of that story was that they were reminded that it was a *game*. All of a sudden, they were playing for the fun and the love of the game. And they won.

O.J. told this story at the Buffalo Bills twentieth-anniversary reunion of O.J.'s 2,000-yard season at the Radisson hotel in Buffalo, New York.

Another story dated back to one of O.J.'s first USC games. The Trojans were playing at Notre Dame. In the last game between the two teams in South Bend before O.J. had joined the Trojans, the Fighting Irish had left the Trojans out on the field in freezing weather for a long time—around fifteen minutes—before the game started. By kickoff, the Trojans were frozen solid. Shivering and demoralized, they just wanted to get the game over with and go home to sunny Southern California.

Afterward, the enraged Trojans coach, John McKay, vowed that would never happen again. So now it's the 1967 season, O.J.'s junior year and rookie season with the Trojans. As the visiting team, USC was expected to take the field first. That's how it's always done. The visiting team takes the field first, *always*.

An official came to the Trojan locker room and told McKay to get his team ready.

"Is Notre Dame out yet?" McKay asked.

The official said, "Home team always comes out last."

McKay told him: "We're not coming out until Notre Dame is on the field."

"Coach, you need to get your team on the field or you forfeit the game," the official retorted dryly.

So McKay turned around and shouted, "Boys, get your uniforms off, we're going home!"

Dumbfounded, O.J. stood there agape. McKay screamed, "Simpson, *get your jersey off, we're going home!*"

The official left and the players started getting undressed. Shortly thereafter, the official came back in. He said, under his breath, "Coach, Notre Dame is on the field."

And McKay beamed a huge smile and hollered, "Boys, get your uniforms on. *It's time to go kick some Irish ass!*"

The players erupted in hoots and screams—so beside themselves with excitement by that time, so pumped up, they went crazy. They already knew they'd won the game—that they'd *mentally* defeated Notre Dame, just as Notre Dame had done to them the trip before. And sure enough, they won. They destroyed Notre Dame 24 to 7, largely because of O.J., who ran for 160 yards and three touchdowns.

O.J. loved telling that one, and we loved hearing it.

When he wasn't regaling us with stories, O.J. spent a lot of time with his attorneys—the Dream Team. He had mixed feelings about them. The team was headed up by the all-star quartet, the Four Horsemen of the legal profession: Robert Shapiro, Johnnie Cochran, F. Lee Bailey, and

Barry Scheck. They were O.J.'s "defensive linemen," as the *Washington Post* called them.

O.J. really wanted Johnnie Cochran to lead his defense. To the very end, he loved and trusted Cochran. When O.J. was arrested, Cochran couldn't immediately join his team because he was busy with another client—Michael Jackson. But O.J. insisted, and he was thrilled when Cochran finally came on board. O.J. ensured that Cochran's role on the team was secure, and he found ways to keep the others from growing resentful or envious. This was a juggling act involving some titanic egos, but O.J. understood how the ego and mind of an alpha male worked, being one himself. He made sure they all felt important while he gradually navigated Cochran to the top position. He was primarily concerned with Shapiro. O.J. said that he felt there was great animosity in L.A. between blacks and Jews. He said that several years earlier, Jewish lenders had given loans to black families against their properties, and when they couldn't make the payments, they would take the homes and businesses and develop the property. For this reason, O.J. was adamant that he did not want Shapiro in front of his mostly black jury. He actually wanted to fire Shapiro, but he was afraid Shapiro would start leaking inside information to the press. So he kept Shapiro around while nudging Cochran to the top dog position.

The two lawyers who wound up hating each other, ironically, began the case as the closest friends: Shapiro and F. Lee Bailey. They had been close for decades, but tension grew during the trial and exploded when both men accused each other of leaking information to the press. The damage was done, and the friendship destroyed. After that blowup, it was total ice and silence between the two. It got very ugly. Shapiro once vowed that he would never work nor speak with F. Lee Bailey again. And, as far as I know, he has kept his word. We found out later that it was Shapiro who leaked the information.

And then there was Bob Kardashian. What can I say about Bob Kardashian that has not been said? A one-time friend and attorney of O.J.'s, he set the original gold standard for O.J. betrayal with his covert, Faustian collaboration with the obese and malodorous Larry Schiller, author of *American Tragedy: The Inside Story of the Simpson Defense*, in which Kardashian provided all kinds of privileged information in order to defame his former friend.

Kardashian is perhaps the only person who betrayed O.J. whose conduct was so offensive and unprofessional that he even earned the scorn of the O.J.-haters *and* the press. You can see everything in the look on his face when the verdict was read. He looked shocked and miserable. I believe he was counting on a guilty verdict—for his book.

About Chris Darden, O.J. was unsparing. "That right there is one motherfucker I would hate to be," he would say. "White people already don't like him because he's black, and now black people hate him because he's an Uncle Tom."

Marcia Clark wasn't his favorite either. I used to get his goat by telling him I found her strangely sexy, especially after her makeover. He said I was sick. "She looks like a wet rat," he'd say.

And then there were the rest of us—O.J.'s friends, colleagues, business associates, confidants, hangers-on, and fellow celebrities. Because of the great mass of media permanently parked outside the jail, nobody could visit O.J. without being tarred and feathered as an O.J. apologist, ally, or even accomplice. Visiting him became a political act in itself. The wives of some of his old buddies threatened divorce if their husbands visited O.J. Being associated with him dealt an immediate and serious blow to people's reputations, businesses, and even marriages. I feel compelled to ask: what would *you* have done?

As the trial progressed and the evidence looked more and more damning against O.J., his visitors started to vanish. Almost everybody from Hollywood disappeared overnight. Marcus Allen only went to visit O.J. once, on that first day when we all went. Of course, as I said, I believe Marcus's role in all this was deep and complex. No wonder he stayed away.

Even Al Cowlings's visits were sporadic. A.C. was a close childhood friend of O.J.'s and a former high school, junior college, USC, Buffalo Bills, and 49er teammate. He drove the infamous white Bronco on June 17. But neither the prosecution nor the defense wanted A.C. to be a witness in the trial, so it served everybody if he just kept away.

The prosecutors didn't want A.C.'s testimony because they knew he'd reveal an incredibly explosive secret: that on June 17 he was driving O.J. to Nicole's grave so that O.J. could commit suicide there. They were afraid that this little-known suicide story might make the jury sympathetic to O.J.—a man grief-stricken over Nicole, who wanted to shoot himself at her grave. They were determined from day one to depict him as a true monster with no feelings whatsoever.

The Dream Team also wanted to keep this story buried and keep A.C. from testifying because he knew O.J. had committed the murders. How on earth could A.C. chauffeur his best friend to his own suicide if not for the fact that, yes, O.J. was guilty of the murders? Additionally, A.C. knew of O.J.'s domestic violence, as it was he who took Nicole to the hospital on New Year's Day, 1989.

The story of O.J.'s aborted suicide attempt is part tragedy, part farce. On June 17, O.J. asked A.C. if they could go for a drive, and they did, in A.C.'s white Ford Bronco. Supposedly, they just wanted to get out of the house. The public believes that A.C. was shocked to discover that O.J. had a gun and was suicidal, and that A.C. called the police to get their help in talking O.J. back to sanity. But in fact, A.C. drove O.J. to Nicole's grave, explicitly so that O.J. could shoot himself there and be reunited with her.

Who told me this?

O.J. did.

He told me during those endless days when he sat in jail signing autographs. He had planned to shoot himself in the head rather than turn himself in. He said he wanted to be with Nicole.

You must remember how important O.J.'s image was to him. He wanted to stop all the sordid details from getting dredged up in a lengthy trial for the world—and above all, for his kids—to see. If he killed himself, he would be a tragic figure—not a hero, but at least the whole affair would have died with him.

They drove to the cemetery and O.J. had the gun that had been given to him years earlier by an NFL executive. A.C. knew O.J. was guilty. Would you take your best friend to kill himself if he were innocent?

During his civil trial, O.J. was asked what he was thinking during that ride.

"I felt at peace that I was going to stop feeling the way I was feeling."

When O.J. and A.C. arrived at the cemetery, they found cops everywhere. They couldn't get in through the front gates. So A.C. took O.J. to the back of the cemetery and wished his friend goodbye. O.J. went off, leaving A.C. in the excruciating position of standing there and waiting to hear the gunshot.

Time passed, but there was no gunshot. Finally, A.C., in agony, approached O.J.

"O.J., Jesus Christ. Are you going to do this or not?"

O.J. retold this story with a hint of black humor.

"Give me a fucking break, man," he recalled saying. "I'm trying to kill myself over here!"

A.C. walked away. Finally, O.J. came back out of the orchard. He had pulled the trigger, he said, but the gun didn't go off.

"I thought this meant I wasn't supposed to do it," he told me. "I remember what my mother always told me, that suicide is a sin, and if you kill yourself you don't go to heaven. I'd never see Nicole again."

So he changed his mind and told A.C. to take him back to Rocking-ham, mainly because he thought his mother was there. But it turned out that Eunice had already left Rockingham. Eunice later made a rare comment to the media. When asked about the Bronco chase and her son's character, she said, "I just don't believe that. O.J. has never been a coward to run. I just think he was wanting to get to me because he thought I could solve the problem."

While A.C. drove O.J. from the cemetery back to Rockingham, he was in contact with the police, telling them he was bringing O.J. home. The famous slow Bronco "chase" on the 405 wasn't really a chase at all. They were just tailing them, almost like an escort. Shortly after he got home, he was taken into police custody.

That's the story neither the prosecutors nor O.J.'s defense team wanted the jury to hear, so A.C. was kept out of the trial.

I have often wondered if O.J. regretted not killing himself that day. Many of us would become suicidal, over time, including myself, from the unrelenting pressures of the trial and the public loathing. If O.J. had committed suicide that day, the entire story would have died with him in the orchard. But that was not his destiny, or ours.

| | | | | | |

O.J. suffered losses in jail that nobody knows about. One that really crushed him was the death of Bobby Chandler. Bobby had played football with O.J. at USC and Buffalo and they were very close friends. Bobby was always the pretty boy, the *GQ* ideal—blond-haired and blue-eyed. He was also a very kind person, and he loved O.J.

Bobby had gotten very severe stomach cramps while watching the Bronco chase on TV. He originally assumed the cramps stemmed from the stress of seeing O.J. in this situation. But the cramps persisted for days, eventually forcing Bobby to the doctor's office. It was stomach cancer. Even after his diagnosis, Bobby continued to visit O.J. in jail. They had been golfing buddies, and if you know golfers, for them, being on the greens was like being in paradise. Bobby would tell O.J. to picture the two of them teeing off in Cabo.

"One year from now, O.J., we'll be up there having a beer, we'll watch the sunset over the ocean, and life will be good again."

But Bobby died in January 1995, just before the trial started. O.J. was devastated.

I often wondered what Bobby would have done when the hard evidence started to come in. You have to understand that O.J.'s friends who believed in his innocence were not bad or stupid people. They were people who knew O.J. To them, it meant something when he said, "I couldn't have done this."

When the hard evidence did start coming in, I remember feeling punched in the stomach. It was just so damning. There were blood drops near the victims' bodies that matched O.J.'s, there were twelve hairs consistent with O.J.'s discovered on the cap found at the crime scene, there was even one of Nicole's hairs, with blood on it, on the glove found at Rockingham.

And then, the DNA evidence began arriving. When it did, I went in to sit with O.J., to lend him support. He looked numb.

"You know, Mike," he said, "it's weird. I watch this DNA evidence...I believe in this stuff. I believe in this science. I look at all this...and I see it and I think I know I had to have done this."

He paused and offered me a vacant look. And then he said, "But Mike, if I did it...wouldn't I remember that I did it?"

Maybe not.

Remember the last time I spoke to O.J. before the murders? He sounded slow, incoherent, and drugged-out. It turns out that he was on Prozac. Why is this relevant?

Dr. Joseph Glenmullen, the author of *Prozac Backlash*, said in an interview for this book, "If O.J. committed these murders while on Prozac, he would remember it like a dream, like something outside of himself, something he saw from above, like an out-of-body experience. He would see it as something somebody else did, not him. It's there in some form in his mind, but not as true memory. It's called a disassociative state. It is the state that people enter right after a gruesome eruption of violence. It's the mind protecting itself. "

Dr. Glenmullen's comments seem to be consistent with O.J.'s. In his 2007 confessional book *If I Did It*, O.J. relayed that after the murders, he found himself standing outside Nicole's house, but "I couldn't remember how I'd gotten there, when I'd arrived, or even why I was there." Then he realized he was covered in blood, and he saw the bloody bodies of Nicole and Ron. "Where the fuck was I when this shit went down?" he asked himself. He said it was "like part of my life was missing—like there was some weird gap in my existence."

Ron Shipp's testimony, too, seems consistent with Dr. Glenmullen's comments. O.J., according to Shipp, admitted to having a dream about killing Nicole and he was worried that that dream might cause him to fail the lie detector test.

And so, it seems possible to me, at least, that when O.J. was on trial he couldn't really remember committing the murders. If you had a gap in your memory, and people were trying to prove that you had committed two brutal murders during that gap, how much evidence would it take before you finally believed them?

Those of us who accepted his guilt, however reluctantly, had trouble explaining what seized him on the night of June 12. But we knew it was something that sprang from hell and grabbed him—something, for once, he couldn't outrun. We knew he was spiraling downward, we knew he was in trouble, especially in the days right before the murders. I sometimes feel as if his circle of friends understood this, understood that O.J. was a victim of something outside his control, but that he could never admit it, partially because O.J. doesn't lose control. He's O.J., remember?

As the trial continued, O.J.'s friends and well-wishers continued to fall away. The betrayals continued to sting.

We were all pretty good people before June 12. Now we are all damaged goods—passably decent people who were left with a series of bad choices, and eventually many of us chose just about all of them. I certainly did. The only person who I can look back and say was stellar is Skip Taft. To this day, Skip has not turned his back on O.J., nor has he ever spoken on the record about the trial.

I remember one day, after the trial had ended, I asked him, "Skip, do you think O.J. would do for us what we just did for him? If the situation were reversed, would he have been there for us?"

"No, Mike," Skip said. "He loves us but he doesn't have the ability to love like you and I do. He wouldn't sacrifice himself for us."

CHAPTER SEVEN

THE GREATEST SHOW
ON EARTH

I got to hear a rare perspective on the trial: O.J.'s. He'd come into the room each day after trial, and I would have either sat through the court proceedings or followed them in the media, and then we'd talk about them as he sat there signing autographs. He would sometimes watch the news of the trial on TV in the hallway outside his cell.

He constantly expressed his own counterpoints to the various testimonies. He'd rant and rave about how biased the media coverage was—and he was right, it was. He complained that the press downplayed anything that went his way, while a bad day for him in court was always headline news.

After the trial ended, O.J. thanked me for staying on as his marketing agent and arranging for him to continue signing autographs to help finance his costly defense. I could have done what most of O.J.'s business associates did—I could have abandoned him as soon as I became convinced of his guilt. But I didn't.

Why not?

We were living in a parallel universe. Inside our bubble, it was as if we could torture the evidence until reality itself was altered. If we closed the windows tight enough, if we filled our minds with myopic interpretations of blood drops and possible scenarios of malfeasance, we could keep the truth monster outside the house. For a little while longer, O.J. could still be the hero he was to me when I was in the eighth grade, and somehow, I could negotiate with the nightmare.

If we could create doubt in the minds of the jurors, we could create doubt in our own minds, and in that space where doubt was created, we could breathe, and we could survive.

I had no formal legal input in O.J.'s defense, but I became part of the larger extra-legal Dream Team offering feedback, financing, and manipulation of public opinion that ultimately, in the hands of the best lawyers in the country, resulted in O.J.'s acquittal. I sat with O.J., day in and day out, throughout the year and a half of his incarceration. I was on the inside looking out, watching the world watch us, and telling O.J. what that world was saying, because he could only watch TV occasionally, and couldn't choose the channel. I was his sounding board and, in many cases, his devil's advocate, telling him what he did not want to hear.

Sometimes I kept my mouth shut and sometimes I gave advice. By virtue of being around O.J. and his legal team so often, I became involved in the defense strategies. I am a fairly cunning person and I harbor a deep-seated sense of distrust and cynicism. This came in handy throughout the trial. The members of the Dream Team were masters of illusion and deception, so I certainly felt right at home. There was nothing we couldn't spin our way, no witness whose credibility we couldn't shred.

It's been said that this was a matter of necessity. And that's true—because, simply put, we didn't have a case. They had the motive, evidence, witnesses, and science on their side. We had nothing. All we could hope to do was weaken their case enough to forge a sliver of reasonable doubt in the minds of the jurors. We inserted that sliver of doubt, not with facts and evidence, but with smoke and mirrors. We put on a play. We manipulated opinion, constantly.

Almost everything you saw from the defense side in that trial was scripted, right down to who was in the courtroom, where they sat, and what color ties the men wore. For example, an expert advised us never to wear a red tie to court on days where blood evidence would be shown, because it could send a subliminal message that we had blood on us. O.J. told me one day, "Mike, if you're coming to court tomorrow, don't wear a red tie, man," and he explained why. O.J.'s ties were chosen according to what feelings and impressions they were said to invoke. On days when there would be testimony about domestic abuse, the rule was not to wear a "power tie," but to choose colors that suggested docility. You could, however, wear a power tie on a day when, for example, Johnnie was going after somebody, shredding him. O.J.'s suits and ties were all numbered and carefully orchestrated; dressing O.J. became its own science.

When O.J. was led from his holding cell into the courthouse each day it was less than twenty-five feet, but I noticed he always, always buttoned his coat, only to unbutton it when he got to the courthouse. I asked him one day: "O.J., why do you always button and unbutton your coat like that?"

He explained that it was to create an appearance of being at ease. "What do you do when you go into a business meeting?" he said. "You unbutton your coat and you sit down." The impression he wanted to create of himself in the courtroom was that of a beleaguered gentleman, expressing, "I am here because I am supposed to be here, and I have to prove my innocence. I am carrying myself with dignity."

Every day he would look over at us in our box, smile, and greet us. Everything he did, the way he carried himself, was studied and deliberate.

One aural memory that will stay with me forever is the sound of Judge Ito's voice saying, "We're back on the record on the Simpson matter." I must have heard that phrase hundreds if not thousands of times. Ito said it at the start of each day, and after every single break and recess, throughout the trial. I can still hear it. "We're back on the record on the Simpson matter." I used to say it in business meetings with O.J. for old time's sake. In fact, every time I sat down to work on this book I would say those words, either to myself or to my editors.

When it came time for the jury to walk through Rockingham, the place had already been refurbished as if by magic elves to influence the jury. It was like changing the set of a play. O.J.'s stairwell wall of photos of him, Nicole, the kids, and rich white friends, were replaced with photos of his black family members and black friends. A bedside photograph of his then girlfriend, the very sexy Paula Barbieri, was replaced with a photo of his mother. They made sure there were fresh-cut flowers everywhere— which made no sense at all, since the owner of the house was in jail. A famous Norman Rockwell painting of a black girl going to school escorted by marshals (about the integration of schools in Little Rock, Arkansas) was taken from Johnnie Cochran's office and hung in O.J.'s house in the central hallway. This "subtle" touch was intended to appeal to the black juror's sense of O.J.'s "blackness." O.J. wound up liking the painting so much that Johnnie let him keep it after the trial was over.

I remember O.J. was angry because the one thing we forgot was to fly the American flag in the yard. He always flew the flag, but that day it was down and nobody remembered to hoist it. He loved being home, even for that short while.

The peak of the magic show was of course around the very damning DNA blood evidence. This is a belabored subject—the DNA evidence— but there are some things worth revisiting.

There was, as you may recall, a trail of blood from Nicole's house to the Bronco and then to Rockingham. Blood was found on the gate at Nicole's, on the Bronco, on the infamous glove, and on one of O.J.'s socks that was found in his bedroom. Genetic fingerprinting as criminal evidence—still in its infancy back then—showed both O.J.'s and Nicole's blood on that sock, as well as the "blue-black" fibers from the clothes O.J. wore that night. These fibers were also found on Ron's shirt and on the glove found at Rockingham. This alone should have convicted O.J. As Mark Fuhrman would later tell me, "It was like the Disneyland of evidence. . . . I couldn't go anywhere without finding evidence. . . . I tried, but wherever I went, there was more evidence."

Here's how we manipulated it—we shifted the focus of attention, planted doubts, and told the audience they weren't seeing what they were actually seeing, just like any good magician would do.

First of all, we leaked the information about the sock to the press, making it look like the prosecution had leaked it. Then we put our own spin on it. The prosecution had video footage from the bedroom that doesn't show a sock on the floor. We stressed this, while omitting the fact that the video was showing a *different* part of the floor from where the sock actually was. Nonetheless, in the confusion, this sowed the idea that the sock could have been planted by the cops.

And we kept going: a sock has four sides, like a towel that you fold in half. We emphasized the fact that three sides of the sock had been soaked through with blood as opposed to two and suggested that this indicated the cops had poured blood on the sock. Of course, we knew that the blood could easily have saturated three surfaces of the sock when O.J. took it off, or if he had stepped on it after he had taken it off.

We then launched a scathing attack on the man who collected the vial of O.J.'s blood at Parker Center (LAPD headquarters). The Dream Team railed about how sloppy the evidence processing was, suggesting the whole time that the blood samples were mishandled and contaminated. We also got a lot of mileage out of the discrepancy between the eight and a half cc of O.J.'s blood the man who took the blood testified to have taken, and the six cc that actually existed. "Where is the missing blood?" the defense demanded to know, thus creating the impression that there *was* missing blood. In truth, we knew that a person drawing blood usually doesn't measure it all that closely. What the man thought was eight and a half cc could easily have been six. What he meant to say is that he drew *about* eight and a half cc. Unfortunately for him, he forgot that one word.

It should have been obvious that if O.J. had nothing to do with the murders, there should never have been any blood at O.J.'s house at all. And yet it was everywhere—his blood *and* the victims'. How would the cops have known that O.J.'s blood was even at the scene? How could they have planted the sock when he was still in Chicago? Our whole argument was absurd.

In undermining the blood evidence, we were helped by the discovery of a few places in the DNA evidence where it seemed possible that blood evidence had, in fact, been planted. There was no blood on Nicole's gate, for example, on the night of the murders when the first pictures were taken. But three weeks later blood was there. It had more of O.J.'s DNA than any other blood they collected, as well as a preservative called EDTA that's used in labs. It was pretty obvious that this blood had been brought from the lab and planted there, which made it easier for us to suggest that all of the evidence was being manipulated. As our expert witness, Dr. Henry Lee, said, "If you find a cockroach in a pot of spaghetti, you don't look for another cockroach before you throw out the whole pot of spaghetti."

The jury did not state that O.J. was "innocent" or that they felt he was "not guilty" of the murders. What the verdict reflected was that the prosecution *did not prove his guilt beyond a reasonable doubt*. The Dream Team created and manipulated that doubt. We especially targeted the black jurors by stressing the possibility that the cops had tampered with the evidence and playing up Mark Fuhrman's alleged use of racist terms.

We all create illusions in order to survive. Most of us just don't do it on this scale.

You know, when I look back on the cast of characters involved in the whole O.J. debacle, one of the very few with whom I'd like to have a beer, whom I respect more today than I did back then, is Mark Fuhrman. He was the key to the whole trial (for both sides) and he ended up being scapegoated by everyone. Was he perfect? No. None of us are. Did he say some things he shouldn't have said? Yes. But so have we all.

In truth, out of all the cops involved in the case, Mark Fuhrman was by far the best. Without the evidence Fuhrman found and collected on the night of the murders, at Bundy and at Rockingham, without the questions he asked, there would not have been a trial. He found the Rockingham glove, the cap, and the bloody fingerprint on the Bundy gate that Vannatter and Lange forgot to collect. He found the blood on the white Bronco while the other cops were simply standing around waiting for backup. The guy was awake, alert—overall an excellent detective.

Marcia Clark and Chris Darden always blamed Fuhrman for their losing the case, but without him they wouldn't have even had a case. The truth of the matter is that Clark and Darden lost the case, not Mark Fuhrman.

O.J. was actually the first person I remember expressing respect for Fuhrman, back when all I could do was look for reasons to tear him down. It was during the preliminary hearing when they were deciding whether there was enough evidence to proceed to trial, and I said to O.J., "There's something about that guy, something very strange." He was so clean, polished, good-looking, well-spoken—like he was auditioning for a movie role. He had bright white starched shirts and everything about him just made him seem a bit too perfect.

As I was griping about how there had to be something sinister about him, O.J. shook his head. "This is a good cop, Mike," O.J. said. "This is a damn good cop. And he is a good witness."

But I was only interested in looking for Fuhrman's faults. We needed to destroy him if we were to have any chance of winning the case. And so we looked and looked for something we could exploit, and then we found it.

I remember the day that we did—I remember it vividly. I went to see O.J. and he was absolutely jubilant. He shot a huge smile at me, and then proceeded to tell me why.

"Mike, man, we got some tapes that are gonna blow this fucking case apart," he said.

"What are you talking about?" I asked.

"We got tapes of Fuhrman saying all kinds of racist shit, about niggers and Mexicans and framing people," O.J. said gleefully.

I pressed him for details and he told me everything he knew about the now infamous Fuhrman tapes. He looked so relieved—like a ton of pressure had just been lifted from his body. His hope had been restored.

From that point on, we knew we had a genuine shot at an acquittal.

An acquittal, though, was still not guaranteed. There was still a lot of evidence to worry about, including the gloves.

This brings me to one of the things I did that I think warrants the hard rap I will take as somebody who helped O.J. get away with murder. This is one of the reasons why my publisher named my book as they did. Here was where I had my best, and worst, idea of the entire trial—O.J. and the glove.

It was a few days before he was going to be asked to try on the gloves in front of the jury, and O.J. was visibly upset.

"I don't want to put them on, Mike," he said. That was understandable. They had Nicole's dried blood all over them, and had been worn by her killer when she was murdered. I was pretty tough on him that day. It wouldn't do him any favors to sugarcoat reality. I took the bull by the horns.

"O.J.," I said, "the jury is going to be watching your every move, your every flinch, everything about your demeanor when you try on those gloves. They're going to want to see how you react. If I were a juror, I would be thinking, 'How would I be feeling if I were innocent of the murders, and had to try on the gloves worn by the man who killed my ex-wife?'"

O.J. shifted in his chair and looked miserable.

Let me wind back a little bit first, and tell you something about these gloves.

O.J. had very large hands. One of the things I remember when I first met him and shook his hand was how small my hand felt in his, like I was a second-grader shaking hands with an adult. When I saw the gloves during the trial, I was fairly sure I recognized them as a pair of gloves I had actually worn myself, when I was with O.J. in Buffalo that preceding football season. We had gone there for a Bills game that O.J. was slated to broadcast for NBC. It was a cold day, and O.J. wore gloves and an overcoat. I remember I was standing under a goalpost, and O.J. handed me his coat and gloves. He needed me to hold them while he put his Bills jersey on over his shirt before participating in a reenactment of the legendary 1973 Shea Stadium game when he broke the 2,000-yard rushing mark. As he ran onto the field, I put the gloves on, admiring their quality and warmth, although they were way too big for me.

"I don't want to wear them, Mike," O.J. said. I felt bad for him. As usual, I tried to think of a solution.

That was when I had the idea. I said, "O.J., what happens when you don't take your arthritis medicine?"

He looked at me, puzzled. "My hands hurt like hell. Why?"

"What else happens?" O.J. was perplexed. He was talking about a serious concern of his and I was asking seemingly irrelevant questions.

"They swell up." O.J. stared at me blankly, still not seeing where I was leading him.

"Exactly," I said, hoping he would finally catch my drift.

O.J. looked at me and I could see the penny drop.

"O.J.," I said very quietly. "Why don't you stop taking your arthritis medicine?"

That was all that needed to be said. O.J. understood. There had been a few times when we were traveling together when he forgot his arthritis medicine and his hands, especially his knuckles, would get huge from swelling.

We didn't discuss it any further. I'm not even sure he ever told his attorneys about our discussion—I don't think they knew.

When he tried on the glove in the courtroom on May 15, with the whole world watching, he said, "It doesn't fit," and made a "gee-whiz" expression. It turned into the iconic moment of the trial, the moment everybody remembers. Those were the only words the jury ever heard O.J. utter.

And Cochran, being a genius, came up with the perfect advertising jingle: "If it doesn't fit, you must acquit."

And they did.

| | | | | |

It was only years later, after the trial was long over, that I started to come apart at the seams. I have already admitted that I never liked Nicole and she never liked me. But she paid me a visit more than once in my dreams, when her ghost appeared, standing right over me, just looking at me. I always tried to tell her I was sorry but could never form any words or sounds. I always woke up in a cold sweat.

I know I created that apparition out of my own guilt-wracked mind. It was as if I were merging into O.J. after all, like I dreamed of doing when I was a kid. Except that I am much weaker than he is.

O.J. was always able to block things out. That's what made him the athlete he was. The Greek definition of tragedy is not that terrible things happen, but the internal measure of what is *felt* about those things. O.J. knew
how to outrun the pain in life. He's running still.

CHAPTER EIGHT

THE ONE
WHO GOT AWAY

There is one person who managed to stay miraculously out of the entire mess, who slipped away quietly into the night, leaving chaos behind him.

I believe Marcus Allen was with Nicole on the day or the evening before the murders. Even if he wasn't, I believe O.J. thought he was. I know that Marcus was seeing Nicole after she and O.J. divorced. I know because Marcus told me.

And I know O.J. knew it, because he told me, too, when he was already behind bars.

I'll tell you the story from my own part of the knot, as agent and friend to both Marcus and O.J. After June 12, I watched one of them go to jail and the other one take off like a jet vanishing above the clouds. I was as clueless as anyone about how it all fit together, about what had happened exactly. The four people who definitely knew about the affair were O.J., Marcus, Nicole, and Nicole's friend Faye Resnick, who was the first one to talk publicly about the affair. Faye said that Nicole was deeply infatuated with Marcus, and that when she spoke to Nicole on June 12, she either had seen or was going to see Marcus again.

Marcus, however, by a stupendous series of dodges, quelled this truth and stamped out the embers of his own critical role in the tragedy.

Here's how I found out about it.

Not long after the murders, Marcus and I were at the Hyatt hotel in Buffalo, New York. Marcus was in town with the Kansas City Chiefs to play the Buffalo Bills, and I had scheduled time for him to do a private autograph session at the hotel. I was in my room when I got a call from a friend. "Mike, you better turn your radio on," he said. Faye Resnick's quickie tell-all book *Nicole Brown Simpson: The Private Diary of a Life Interrupted* had come out that week. "Apparently she says in there that she and Nicole were walking on the beach when Nicole pointed to a piece of driftwood and told her that Marcus's penis was like a big piece of driftwood."

"*What?*"

"And this radio station is holding a contest. Whoever brings in the biggest piece of driftwood wins tickets to the game; then they're going to burn the pile of driftwood at Rich Stadium."

"You've got to be kidding me."

He added that the story wasn't just on the radio station, it was in the tabloid press too.

I was sickened and outraged. I knew the station—it was the one licensed to broadcast the Buffalo Bills's home games. I immediately called one of the top executives in the Bills organization and told him what "their" station was doing. I said it was disrespectful to Nicole, to Marcus, and to O.J.

Then I dashed down to the hotel gift shop and sure enough, there on the news rack were the tabloids with Marcus's photo and articles about Resnick's book. Two men were laughing at the cheesy picture on the cover and discussing asking Marcus to autograph the tabloid. I grabbed every copy I could find.

"You got any more behind the counter?" I asked the clerk.

"No, sir," she said nervously.

I brought the newspapers up to my room and threw them in the closet. I didn't want people who were coming to get Marcus's autograph to see the scandalous headlines—or to ask Marcus to autograph them.

About an hour later, Marcus came to my room to go over some paperwork. I didn't say anything about the newspapers. As he was leaving, he looked over, and saw the big stack of tabloids.

"What's all that?"

I said nothing.

He picked one up. There was dead silence before he left the room.

He called me a while later and I went to his room for dinner. He wanted to talk. He said, "You know it wasn't like that, right, Mike?"

"Wasn't like what?"

"It wasn't like what's in here."

"You *didn't* have an affair with Nicole?"

"No."

"So you never had sex with Nicole?"

"No, we never made love."

I stared at him. I didn't like the evasiveness of his answer.

"So," I said carefully, "*you never had sex with Nicole?*"

He hesitated. "We had oral sex and stuff like that, but we never made love."

"Oh, well, that's okay," I said sarcastically.

"Mike, I went over, just trying to stay in touch with her, so that she'd know we were still her friends even though she was divorced from O.J. One thing led to another. . . . I didn't mean for it to happen."

I was really taken aback. Until that day, I'd had no idea it was true. All I knew was that prior to Resnick's book, Marcus had categorically denied having sex with Nicole. Not long after the murders, prosecutor Chris Darden asked him, "Did you ever have a sexual relationship with Nicole?"

Marcus said, "No."

Based on what Marcus personally told me, I am convinced that was a lie, and he was under oath. There was no turning back after that. When Marcus denied the relationship to Darden, I think he assumed the whole matter would die right there. And without Resnick's book, it might have.

Now that I knew, Marcus seemed eager to talk about it, to explain or rationalize it to me.

"It's just amazing how quickly life can turn on you," he said somberly. "Mike, everything was just great for all of us not long ago. My career was going great. Things were going great for O.J., for you, for all of us. Now look at us. Nicole's been murdered. O.J.'s in jail. A.C. may be thrown in jail. I'm on the cover of a tabloid. Look at us now."

I thought it was high time O.J. knew the truth about Nicole and his friend, a man I had thought much better of until now, a man who was, in fact, one of my own closest friends. As soon as I got back to L.A., I went to see O.J. in jail.

"O.J., I need to tell you something."

"Okay, what is it?"

I told him what Marcus told me.

"So he admitted it to you?"

I was stunned that O.J. already knew. "He said they had oral sex and stuff like that, but didn't make love."

"What do you mean *stuff like that*?"

"I don't know, O.J. I was kind of shocked. I didn't press him for details."

"You need to talk to Johnnie [Cochran]. We need Marcus to come forward and admit that shit in court."

"Why?"

"Because the prosecution will try to make it look like I was so jealous I killed Nicole over Marcus or Goldman. He needs to testify that I was cool about it."

O.J. then told me the backstory. He said Nicole had confessed to him in tears that she'd been seeing Marcus, and that she wanted O.J. to make Marcus back off. She was upset that Marcus was treating her poorly, dropping by for "booty calls."

According to O.J., he called Marcus and said, "Marcus, Nicole told me everything. You've got to stop calling her. Just be cool."

"O.J., what are you talking about?"

"Marcus, Nicole told me everything."

On the phone, Marcus insisted that nothing had happened, but a few days later, according to O.J., "Marcus comes over and he's crying. 'I'm so sorry, man, one thing led to another. . . . I'm sorry.' I said, 'Marcus, listen, Nicole and I are divorced. What I'm disappointed in is that you never told me that Nicole wanted to get back together with me. She told you that. She told me so. We're SC guys, man, we don't do shit like this to each other.'"

Now O.J. wanted *me* to persuade Marcus to come clean.

"Mike, you got to go to Kansas City and talk to your boy. This isn't about Marcus getting into the fucking Hall of Fame. I didn't tell Marcus to fuck my ex-wife. This is about the possibility of me never getting out of jail or seeing my kids again." He pleaded with me, "Come on, Mike."

I was in an excruciating position. I was torn between two of my close friends and clients. Marcus was the guy I always thought would put my kids through college if I suddenly died. He was that kind of person in my life. Now O.J. was pressuring me very hard to do something I didn't want to do. They were both my clients and friends. I truly loved Marcus. To this day I mourn the loss of his friendship.

I knew I had to do what O.J. asked, even though I dreaded it. I flew to Kansas City to talk to Marcus. We met at the Crowne Plaza hotel.

After hearing me out, he replied, "I'm not going to testify. You're going to have to tell O.J. that if I testify I'm going to have to be honest and tell the whole thing. If they ask me if I ever saw O.J. stalk Nicole, I would have to say yes. I would have to tell them that he was with me when he yelled for me to pull my car over, ran into the bushes, and peered into a restaurant window to see who Nicole was with and what she was doing."

He looked at me and said, "Mike, just because O.J. didn't get pissed off at me about me and Nicole, doesn't mean he didn't kill her."

That was true. Marcus was in a hell of a position, as was I.

I remember saying to Marcus, "If this is the truth, and this is why you don't want to testify, I accept it. Then don't testify. But if it's to cover your ass or protect your image, reputation, or marriage you need to do the right thing and tell the truth."

That was the end of the conversation.

I flew back to Los Angeles and told O.J. what Marcus had said, that "He would have to be honest, O.J."

"That's what I want, for him to be fucking honest."

Haltingly, I went on: "He said he saw you stalking Nicole."

"*When the fuck did Marcus Allen see me stalk fucking Nicole?*"

"O.J., don't get pissed at *me*. I went to Kansas City to talk to Marcus because you asked me to, and this is what he said."

"Then fucking let him tell them about the stalking. I need him to testify that I was cool when he told me about the affair, which he knows is the truth."

"I can't take this. You know what? *You* tell him. I'll set up the call."

I arranged a conference call between the two of them. Shortly after the scheduled call took place, both of them were calling both of my numbers. I spoke to O.J. first. He was furious. He relayed the conversation, more or less yelling.

"I said, 'Marcus, you got to come clean.' He starts playing stupid. 'What do you mean come clean, O.J.?' I said, 'About your affair with Nicole, Marcus.' He said, 'I can't do it, *because it never happened.*' I said, '*Excuse me?* Who the fuck is there with you? Is somebody on the line with you? Is Kathryn there? Your lawyer? Marcus, *we both know it happened.* I need you to come out and say that you had an affair with Nicole.'"

O.J. ranted a bit longer. Eventually I signed off and called Marcus back. When I spoke to Marcus, he said, "O.J. wants me to lie for him and say I had an affair with Nicole."

"Marcus, you told *me* you had the affair."

He said nothing.

That's was when I lost respect for him. I was so shocked that Marcus would lie to me and do that to O.J. And, as far as I know, that was the last time O.J. and Marcus ever spoke.

I had a strained relationship with both of them after that. I felt Marcus should have been honest about the affair, although I understood that he was locked in by his denial to Chris Darden. He was also right that O.J.'s being cool about the affair didn't mean that he was innocent of the murders. Marcus clearly believed that O.J. was guilty. He told me once, "Mike, O.J. couldn't *look* at me in jail. Couldn't look me in the eyes."

And I understood why O.J. was so furious after that phone call. Marcus did have an affair with Nicole. Nicole had told him so, Marcus had told him so, and now he was saying, "It didn't happen."

I still represented Marcus for a few more years, but the whole incident weighed on us and frayed our friendship.

The day before Marcus was going to be deposed in the civil trial in 1996, I was at Rockingham. Dan Leonard, one of O.J.'s lawyers, started grilling me about Marcus. I told Dan, "Don't use me as a pawn to get to Marcus. I love Marcus."

He said, "Mike, I need information from you." At that moment, O.J. walked in.

"Mike, man, you got to talk to Dan."

They sat on either side of me, and O.J. demanded I tell Dan everything I knew about Marcus and Nicole's affair.

"Talk to Marcus. All I know is what he told me."

"No. Fuck that. Fuck Marcus," O.J. told me. "He's a lying motherfucker. You got to sit down and *talk to Dan*. And Marcus has got to tell the truth. It's not your fault that he lied to Christopher Darden."

I gave in. I told Dan Leonard everything that had transpired, and he took careful notes.

Marcus was deposed the next day, and still denied the affair, adamantly, under oath.

Marcus, over the years, has done everything possible to avoid subpoenas: from slipping away on long vacations, to changing hotels, to traveling with a personal bodyguard, to hiding in the backseat of cars with darkened windows (which is how he got to and from practices), to all sorts of other dodges. I heard that his wife, Kathryn, said to him at a party once, when they were arguing over yet another subpoena, "Marcus, if you don't have anything to hide, why are you running all the time?"

They are no longer married.

Here is what Marcus said in his deposition in the civil trial, under oath:

> Q. Did you ever have a romantic relationship with Nicole?
> A. No, I did not.

Q. Did Nicole and you, for example, ever kiss one another romantically?

A. No, I did not.

Q. So, no kind of sexual or romantic involvement did you ever have with her?

A. None whatsoever.

Q. Did she ever express to you romantic feelings that she had for you?

A. No, she did not.

Q. And did you ever express such feelings to her?

A. No, I did not.

Q. Your relationship with Nicole was purely one of friendship and nothing more?

A. Yes, it was.

Q. Did you make that clear to Mr. Simpson?

A. Yes. I think he understood that.

Marcus described how he and O.J. had been close friends since 1978. Then came a noteworthy exchange:

Q: Now, you have indicated to me that your relationship with Mr. Simpson is different now than it was for all these years, true?

A: Yes, it is.

Q: And it changed when?

A: Well, the—I think one phone call—I think he wanted me to write a letter in opposition to an article that I think *Time* magazine had written, and I didn't do that. And I think secondly he also wanted me to testify to a conversation that we allegedly had—well, excuse me, a conversation that we had in reference to my admitting to him or something of that— you know, the fact about a relationship with his ex-wife, and the conversation, it wasn't true. The relationship didn't happen. And, so, I think he got upset with me, and obviously I felt—really—I felt really sort of—I was in a tough position, and I think thereby the conversation never took place again. I am sure he was disappointed, and I was sort of disappointed too, that I couldn't help him as a friend, but I couldn't go there and say these things because they didn't take place.

Marcus was also questioned about his relationship with me:

Q. How long have you known Mike Gilbert?

A. Awhile. A long time.

Q. And how would you describe your relationship with Mr. Gilbert?

A. I think it's a good relationship.

Q. (By Mr. Leonard) You—over the period of time that you knew Mr. Gilbert, did you become friendly with him?

A. Yes.

Q. And he handled some of your public relations and promotional activities, correct?

A. Specifically—specifically card shows. That was basically it.

Q. Okay. And you would from time to time travel—he would travel with you or would meet you in locations to—
A. Yes.

Q. You have to let me finish.
A. Oh, I am sorry. I thought you were done. I apologize.

Q. —when you would go to card shows?
A. Are you done?

Q. Yeah.
A. Yes.

Q. Okay. Do you believe Mr. Gilbert to be an honest person?
A. I think he is.

Q. Have you ever had any occasion to—where you knew that Mr. Gilbert was lying?
A. No. I don't think so. I think he is a pretty honest guy.

Q. And you had trusted him to assist you in your business enterprises to some extent, correct?
MR. PETROCELLI: Objection. Leading and misstates his testimony.
A. Yes.

Q. (By Mr. Leonard) Okay. And why is it that you no longer have a business relationship with Mr. Gilbert?

A. I think because of all that have—that has happened, Mike, I guess he was under a lot of strain, and he had said he had gotten several death threats, and stuff, for I guess his working relationship with O.J., and he decided it was time to get out of business. I think he put his family before, you know, everything else, I guess.

Q. And is that something that Mr. Gilbert told you, that he was getting out of the business and no longer wanted to have a relationship with you? Is that your testimony?
A. With me?

Q. Yeah.
A. I didn't—I don't think he said he didn't want to have a relationship with me. He just said he couldn't—you know, he was moving on, he was getting out of this business. It was too stressful under the circumstances.

There were other lurid details that emerged during the criminal trial. Jason, O.J.'s son from his first marriage, was dropping something off for Sydney and Justin at Nicole's house one day. Jason had called Nicole to let her know he was stopping by. When he pulled up in front of Nicole's condo, Marcus was racing out of her house with his shirt untucked, carrying his shoes. Jason said he never thought anything of it, because it would never occur to him to suspect an affair.

The conversation that I had with Marcus on June 13 made sense finally, after all these pieces came together. Virtually the first thing he said when we got on the phone was: "Are they mentioning me ... in the media? Have you heard anything about me?"

"Marcus, why would they mention *you*?"

That comment, in retrospect, always made me believe Marcus was there that night.

Then, after he said that, he blindsided me with the news that he would not be returning to L.A. for Nicole's funeral, which just made my head spin.

At least now I can make sense of it.

I have no proof, but my belief is that if it weren't for Marcus Allen's relationship with Nicole, June 12 would have come and gone like any other summer night in Brentwood—and that Nicole and Ron would still be alive.

CHAPTER NINE

NICOLE AND ME

I don't know why I never bonded with Nicole, it may have been because we had different investments in O.J.; we wanted different things. We had a conflict: I was the person who always took him away for professional obligations—signings and appearances—and it meant he was often away from Nicole and the kids. Nicole resented it, and probably resented me. I remember one time when I had driven to Brentwood from Hanford—a three-hour drive—to do a signing with O.J. at Rockingham. He had completely forgotten about it, and so I called him at Nicole's. He apologized profusely and asked me to just bring the stuff over to Bundy and he would sign it there. Nicole blew a gasket. I could hear her in the background, yelling at O.J. It was family night. I understood that, but I had driven three hours and this was only going to take about an hour of his time. She wouldn't budge. So I drove all the way back to Hanford with the stuff unsigned in the trunk, fuming.

It happened another time. O.J. and I were in negotiations, believe it or not, for a fund-raiser to benefit a center for abused women. They wanted him very badly, and were going to pay us $25,000. I was also negotiating a private autograph signing for the same amount. We were set to make $50,000 in one day. He came back to me and said Nicole didn't want him to do it.

"*What*?" I said. "They're sending a private plane for you. You'll be back in L.A. by nightfall. It's an easy gig."

"Nope. Can't do it. I promised Nicole we'd take the kids to the zoo that day."

"Can't you guys go to the zoo the next day?"

I was incredulous. But it was hopeless. The answer was no, because Nicole said so.

I got a little testy with her that time. I said to her, "You know, Nicole, you have no concept of money. I don't have a bottomless checkbook or platinum card. I have to work for a living."

She just shrugged it off and said, "We're going to the zoo, period."

I don't know if they ended up at the zoo or not but we lost $50,000 for a day's work.

Speaking for myself, and not for anybody else who worked for O.J., I felt we were making her lifestyle possible by making sure O.J. upheld his professional commitments and kept making money. Nicole hardly ever worked a day in her life after the time she was a teenage waitress. That was when O.J. met her and they fell in love. O.J. felt she should have been more grateful for the lifestyle he gave her—she lived in luxury, as did her entire family, thanks to O.J. Everything she had was because of him: the luxury condos, the cars, the vacations, everything. I tended to agree with him on this. When he railed and complained about Nicole, I was not one to defend her. Now I wish I had—among many of the things I wish I could change.

I think she started out as a very good person but she became corrupted, spoiled.

In 1994, O.J. was one of NBC's commentators for the Super Bowl in Atlanta. Nicole had tickets for a group of us to go to the game together.

She was staying at the Ritz-Carlton, so the plan was for her to meet me in the lobby. I called when I was on my way. I called when I got there. She kept saying she needed more time, ten more minutes, ten more minutes. Finally she said, "Just come up to the room." I let the cab go, and went up. She was just stepping out of the tub and was wrapped in a towel. She certainly was not shy, and she was definitely not apologetic. She handed me the ticket and I thanked her. She said, "Don't thank me, thank O.J."

Nicole either loved you or hated you, and I was not one of her favorite people.

Many who worked for O.J. had a problem with Nicole. She treated us dismissively and sometimes even with hostility. I think that was due to her problems with O.J. more than anything to do with us. But she was certainly not warm to me or Cathy Randa, or Michelle, the housekeeper. O.J. loved to talk about how Nicole had once socked Michelle on the jaw for no reason other than that Michelle infuriated her with her mere presence at Rockingham. O.J. stopped Michelle from filing a police report, but couldn't stop her from resigning. Her replacement, Gigi, fared no better.

Nicole, when she was in her mode of "stalking" O.J. after their separation, would march into Rockingham and try to get access to his office. She would try to give orders to Gigi. When Gigi would not obey her, saying, "I don't work for you, I work for O.J.," Nicole would become enraged.

In retrospect I realize how angry and flustered Nicole became after she was unseated as O.J.'s wife, after she and the kids left Rockingham. In that last year before her death, she wanted to move back to Rockingham even more than she wanted to get back together with O.J. Home and family and stability meant everything to her. She hated being alone and single. She hated losing the extended circle of family and friends, the holidays, the parties, and the barbecues she had enjoyed for so many years at Rockingham.

O.J. met Nicole, remember, when she was eighteen years old and a waitress at a place he used to go to called The Daisy. She was blond, beautiful, and charming—and she had no idea who he was. Her idol was Roger Daltrey. O.J. liked her innocence.

When O.J. and Nicole met, he was unhappily married to his first wife, Marguerite, who was pregnant with their third child. He used to claim that Marguerite "tricked" him with that pregnancy, which tells you a lot about the man's immaturity and narcissism. He was just annoyed because he was ready to leave her and the baby was getting in his way. I never met Marguerite, but I've heard she felt totally overshadowed and erased by O.J.

Marguerite was always described as "conservative and staid"—the polar opposite of Nicole, who was explosive and impulsive, just like O.J.

O.J. felt he was on his way to the top and Marguerite was an impediment. He had already set up Nicole in an apartment when Marguerite gave birth to the baby O.J. never wanted Marguerite to have—a girl named Aaren. Aaren drowned at the age of two in the family swimming pool. She was in a coma for a few days before she died, and there are conflicting stories about whether O.J. came tearing down the hospital corridor screaming at Marguerite that she had "killed" his child. I hope that's not true, but it sounds just like him. Everything is self-pity and blame unto others.

It took me many years to realize that he has no empathy for any other human being. The story about Aaren's death was always a matter of how "crushed" O.J. was—never what it might have been like for poor Marguerite, whom O.J. abandoned to take up with Nicole. In some media it was reported that when Marguerite was married to O.J., she made more than a few calls to the police, was frequently black and blue, and wore dark glasses regardless of whether it was sunny. She raised their two kids—Arnelle and Jason—quietly and with dignity, and never spoke a word to the public about her marriage to O.J. I bet she wished she had stuck with her original suitor: O.J.'s mild, kind, warm-hearted, and long-suffering best friend, Al Cowlings.

In the years since Nicole was murdered, I have not once heard O.J. express grief over her death or empathy for her suffering or horror over what happened to her. But I did hear O.J. tell jokes about Nicole's death. Once, in jail, I was sitting with him and I had a newspaper with me. "Check the horoscope," he said. I turned the pages to the horoscope page. "Check Taurus. Does it say 'Hey, *I'm dead*'?"

I could not believe he had said that. Nicole was a Taurus.

Another joke that tore him up was about Ronald Reagan. "Mike, Ronald Reagan wants to have lunch with me and Nicole."

"With you and Nicole? I don't understand what you mean."

"Mike, Reagan has Alzheimer's, remember? He doesn't remember that Nicole is dead." He told that "joke" to me more than once.

That's not what you'd expect to hear from a man talking about the love of his life. But the true love of O.J.'s life was O.J.

◀ *Here I am with O.J. in his backyard on the day his divorce from Nicole was finalized in October 1992.*

▼ *O.J. and my son Luke not long after O.J. was acquitted of the murders. He didn't leave the house much in the months following the acquittal, in part because his house was under siege by reporters. He set up a golf net at home, and we played a game we called "Neighborhood Golf." We would miss the net on purpose, and the winner was the first person to get a yell from one of the horde of reporters.*

▲ *Here is O.J. with my grandmother in 2002, not long before she died. My grandmother was sick, and O.J. really wanted to do something nice for her. He took the three-hour trip to Hanford to meet her. We stopped at an antique store where O.J. found this lamp. He presented it to her, plugged it in for her, and showed her how to turn it on and off. I will always be grateful to him for being so kind. This was the side of O.J. that I knew outside of the murders.*

▲ *Here is my son David with O.J. and Bob Costas on the set of* NFL Live! *in the fall of 1993.*

▲ *A typical Christmas sometime in the late eighties: O.J. gave Nicole this fur coat and stacks of cash.*

▲
◀ *Nicole in the early years of their courtship and marriage.*

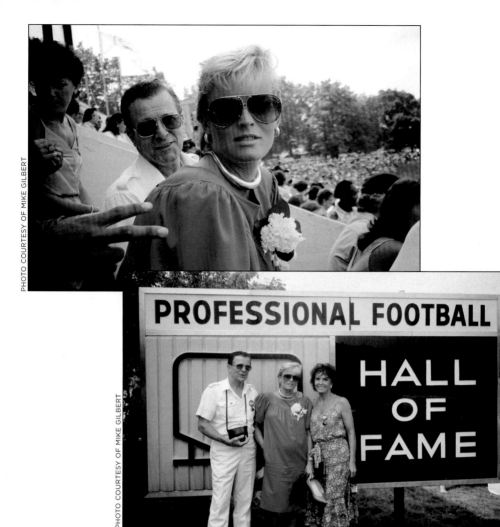

▲ *Here are Nicole and her parents at the NFL Hall of Fame for O.J.'s induction ceremony in 1985. She was pregnant with Sydney.*

◀ *Here I am with O.J. at a lithograph signing about a year before the murders. The lithograph he signed that day hung on the wall in Nicole's house.*

▲ *Moving Day, January 1996. O.J. was forced to sell his New York condominium to help pay for legal expenses. Because there were a lot of Nicole's personal items in the apartment, O.J. did not want strangers packing up her things, and he also feared they would tip off the press. He asked me to do it personally. It took me and my brother Larry three days to move everything out.*

▲ *O.J.'s treasured Ferrari—another possession he lost after the murders.*

▲ *O.J. on the day of his not guilty verdict. He gave me the "lucky" suit he wore that day. O.J. was looking for this suit when he broke into the sports memorabilia collection at a Las Vegas casino in September 2007.*

▲ *I now own, along with two associates, Al Cowling's Bronco from the famous chase. We purchased it to keep it from being used in non-tasteful ways. I took this photo of the Bronco at the lot in southern California where we store it. It still sits there today. In fact, the Bronco has only been driven once in the last fourteen years.*

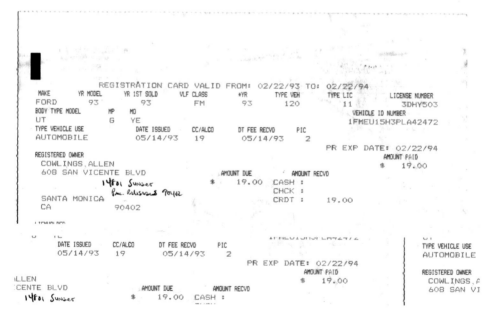

▲ *Al Cowling's Bronco registration. Many people thought the Bronco from the slow-speed chase and the Bronco seized at Rockingham were the same vehicle, but the Bronco seized because of the blood found in, on, and near the vehicle belonged to O.J., and the Bronco used in the slow-speed chase was Al Cowling's.*

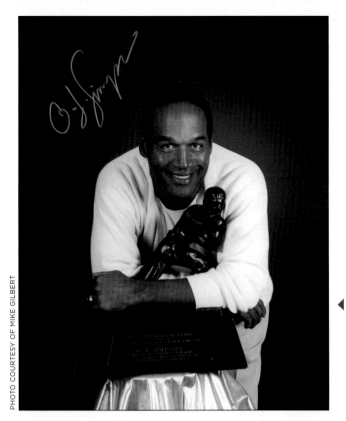

◀ *This photograph was taken, printed, and autographed on the one-year anniversary of the not guilty verdict, October 3, 1996. This was the last time O.J. was photographed with his Heisman trophy.*

▲ *Here I am with O.J. and Skip Taft, O.J.'s lawyer, on the one-year anniversary of the not guilty verdict.*

▲ *Here I am with O.J. about four years ago at The Palms Casino Resort in Las Vegas.*

▼ *O.J. at work, signing jerseys during the same trip to Las Vegas.*

This is me on Lost Arrow Spire—the ▶
rock I was supposed to climb on the
day of the murders—in Yosemite
National Park. I was finally able to
return and climb it on my fiftieth
birthday, three years ago.

CHAPTER TEN

THE VERDICT AND HOMECOMING

T he trial had wrapped, and it was time for the jury to deliberate. We assumed the jurors would need at least two or three weeks to reach a verdict, and we planned our lives accordingly. The jury began their deliberations on October 2, 1995.

I was getting ready to pick up a thousand photographs for O.J. to sign that day. All of a sudden Skip's assistant, Judy, came running down the hall crying out, "They have a verdict!"

"*Who* has a verdict?"

"*O.J.'s jury* has reached a verdict."

After only three and a half hours. I looked over at Skip, who was ashen. I took hold of his arm. "Mike, this isn't good," he said. "This isn't good."

Skip walked over to the TV in his office and turned it on. There it was, all over the news: The verdict would be delivered the next morning.

I tried to reassure Skip. "Think about it. They're not going to put O.J. in prison for the rest of his life after three and a half hours of deliberation. The jury would ask themselves if they believe any evidence was planted in this case. Skip, if they say yes, then they have to let O.J. go. They have to."

Skip said, "I need to get to the jail. O.J. is going to be in a panic."

We drove separately to the jail, which was swarming with media hordes. I remember walking down the gray concrete walkway and hearing reporters (some of whom I'd gotten to know, having seen them every day for the last year and a half) call out, "Mike! Mike! I need to talk to you!" But I just kept moving through what felt like a dream. It was as if I were on a conveyor belt, whisking past everyone else, while I kept my focus on the glass doors of the jail. I got there and signed in. Somebody said O.J. was in his usual room. They closed the metal door behind me, then the next one. In that moment I focused on making my demeanor strong and upbeat. I made my way into the attorney room. O.J. was off to one side. Skip was already there, as was Bob Kardashian, who unbeknownst to us had sold O.J. out in a book deal with Larry Schiller. Cathy Randa's attorney was there too.

Everybody was talking about scenarios. The one possibility—that the verdict would be "guilty"—didn't necessitate any planning, nor was it ever mentioned. That's not to say it didn't weigh very heavily, silently, in all our minds. It certainly did in mine. But we avoided mentioning it, speaking the words. The other possibility—"not guilty"—would require careful planning, so we threw ourselves into that.

The questions were how to get O.J. out of there and where to take him. F. Lee Bailey had offered a private jet to fly O.J. wherever he wanted to go. A few of us, myself included, were pushing for him to fly to Maui and stay at the Ritz-Carlton until the madness died down a little. He wanted to see Sydney and Justin right away,* but they were in the custody of the Brown family, so that too was complicated.

Then O.J. said he wanted to make a statement to the press outside the courthouse if he were acquitted.

At that moment the lieutenant at the jail came over and asked if he could talk to me outside. "Sure," I said, and we went out into the lobby.

"Listen," he said. "O.J. is under the impression that if the verdict goes his way he can just walk out of the courthouse and address the media on the steps, like Perry Mason. It doesn't work like that."

"Okay," I said. "Then how does it work?"

"If he is found guilty he will immediately be transported to a holding facility until they figure out which prison to send him to."

"Okay."

"If he is found not guilty he will still have to be transported back to the jail and then processed out. His possessions will be boxed up and returned to him, and he will be released like all other inmates. I'll show you. Follow me."

He walked me through the maze of the jail to show me the exit from which O.J. would be released.

"I would suggest that you folks get a few different vehicles."

"Okay. But O.J. still wants to make a statement."

"That is not a good idea. We don't want that."

"Why not?"

"We have received numerous death threats against O.J. People have said that if he is found not guilty they will shoot and kill him as he leaves this jail. For that reason, we will most likely have SWAT teams stationed around these buildings to make sure he is safe. As long as he is on this property, he is still our responsibility. We would like him to get off the property as quickly and quietly as possible."

I felt stunned. It is a feeling I would experience countless times in the years to come. This was my very first inkling that O.J. would not be welcomed back into the community with open arms.

I went back into the visiting room and started listening again to the clamor of plans. Various people were offering limos, vehicles, planes, and

---

* Arnelle and Jason had been able to visit O.J. in jail. He had not seen Sydney and Justin since he arrived at jail.

houses. The only one who didn't seem interested in any of this was O.J. At one point he hushed us. He raised his arms and said, "Guys, guys, slow down. This could all be *moot*. This could all be a moot fucking point. *We don't know* what the verdict is."

At that, everybody just kind of stopped. Skip broke the silence. "O.J., don't think like that."

"But it's true. We don't know."

Some people have claimed that O.J. knew what the verdict was going to be. That is nonsense—he had no idea.

I asked him what Johnnie Cochran had said about the extremely short deliberation time.

"He thought it was good, but he said it could still go either way. Nobody knows."

I told O.J. about my conversation with the lieutenant.

"Death threats? What the fuck are you talking about? This is crazy. Why are people talking like this?"

"O.J., you can't make a statement. If you get shot, they'll have the L.A. riots all over again."

He shook his head in disbelief.

"Anyway, if you're found not guilty, they're going to take you back to the jail. They have to process you out, the way they do any other inmate."

"Mike, if I'm found not guilty there's no way I'm going back to that fucking cell."

"You're not going back to the cell. They'll hand you your things and we'll get out of there as quickly as we can. And we'll have several cars."

"When am I going to see my kids?"

I told him I had no idea but that I understood it was his first priority.

O.J. told us all, "Listen, guys, if I'm found not guilty, I want to go *home*. I don't want to go to Maui. I don't want to go to Florida. I want to go *home*. I have not even been able to grieve for Nicole. I want to go back to the home we shared, and grieve, and start my life over. I want to see my kids. Just let me go home."

Everybody went quiet.

I said, "Whatever you say, O.J. It's your decision. Just understand, the press will *surround* your house."

"I understand that. I still want to go home."

So that was that.

It was close to 8:00 PM, the end of visiting hours. Skip and I were the last ones still there with O.J.

O.J. put his hand up to the glass partition. He said, "I want you both to know that I love you. I never could have gotten this far without you. If the verdict is guilty, I never want to see you guys again. I wouldn't want to burden you with having to come visit me. I wouldn't have anything to offer, anything to share with you. I'm serious, guys. Don't come back if the verdict is guilty. Don't come back ever."

I looked at him, and wondered if this could be the very last time I ever saw him. The guards said we had to get going.

My last words to him were, "I love you, man. I'll see you tomorrow at Rockingham."

They came to take him back to his cell and I remember the sound of the chains rattling against the metal chair, a sound I prayed I would never have to hear again. They led him out of the room and we watched him disappear through the doors. I turned away. I was crying, and so was Skip. We went out to the middle room, and before we exited I said to Skip, "Hang on a second. Let's not go out yet. We can't go out there looking like we've been crying." We found tissues and dried our eyes. We each took a deep breath and walked out. The press surrounded us instantly. I didn't want to say anything, and I definitely didn't want them to see my face because even though I had dried my eyes it was pretty obvious I had been crying pretty hard. I dodged left and found a path to get away. I'd already learned that if you moved quick enough, you could escape from the television reporters because their cameramen were loaded down with their bulky equipment.

I looked back over my right shoulder and saw Skip trapped in a blaze of camera lights. I was thinking about how hard it must have been for him, because Skip loved O.J. and had been his friend and attorney for more than twenty years, much longer than I had known O.J.

I kept going. I had to let him fend for himself. But I felt bad, like I had deserted a buddy in battle and allowed him to be surrounded by the enemy.

I got to my car and drove off as fast as I could. I went to my room at the Hyatt. My cell phone was ringing nonstop. I answered it once and it was CNN. They asked if they could film my reaction over at Rockingham as the verdict was read. I said, "No way."

I turned off my cell phone and the hotel phone, and took an Ambien to help me fall asleep. It had no effect. I took another half. Still no effect; I was wide awake. I finally got up and started getting dressed. I decided to drive home. I was afraid of how I would react emotionally if I were in the courtroom for the verdict. If he were found guilty, I didn't want to watch people celebrate my friend having to go to prison for the rest of his life. It wasn't the smartest move I ever made—driving home after taking a dose and a half of Ambien—but I drank a lot of coffee, drove at a steady, good speed, and before I knew it, I was home.

I got there about twenty minutes before they read the verdict. The kids were at school. Debbie had the TV on and a few relatives had come over.

I stood still in front of the TV, mentally bracing myself for whatever verdict came down. I remember hearing the first "not guilty." I sucked in a gasp of air and said, "Wait, it's not over yet." I wanted to wait until all the verdicts were read. They continued to repeat "not guilty" all the way through. I had a slightly delayed reaction, like an echo. Then I saw O.J.

mouth the words "thank you" to the jury and saw Johnnie's reaction; that was when it hit me.

Every phone in the house started ringing off the hook. It was pandemonium. Everybody from my entire life was calling. Neighbors were knocking on the door, people were walking right into the living room, sharing their reactions and asking me questions about what O.J. had said and felt the day before. They were all very upbeat. I was dazed and stunned.

I sat down and just absorbed the moment, took stock. I remember feeling at the time that I had done the right thing by sticking by him, and that now we could go on with our lives. Debbie gave me a very long hug, not a celebratory hug but more of an *it's finally over* hug.

From the moment I had called home from Yosemite on June 13, 1994, to this one, almost a year and a half later, our entire lives and consciousnesses had been dominated by this ordeal. I was worried about the toll it had taken on my family. But truthfully, back then my first instinct was always to worry about O.J. Later, when the cracks in my marriage started to manifest, it was, as with almost everything else in this hideous ordeal, too late to save it.

I drove to my kids' school and took them out of class to tell them the news. They already knew. Luke and Lindsay had big smiles on their faces.

"Dad, we watched the verdict on TV in the classroom," Luke told me. I laughed a little. He asked, "Does this mean that Uncle O.J. can come home now?"

"Yes, sweetheart," I said. "It does."

I knew I had to drive back to L.A. and get to Rockingham by nightfall, but first I had some business to attend to. I had had O.J. sign one thousand envelopes in jail, and my brother-in-law John had agreed to help me get them ready for the post office to turn them into caches (envelopes that are stamped and cancelled by the post office to verify their postage date). My brother-in-law was licking stamps on the entire three-hour drive to

L.A., and then we had to wait in line at the post office in downtown Los Angeles to have each of them cancelled. I never wound up selling those, and still have them. I have received so many macabre offers from people for O.J.-related objects they wanted to buy for various commercial or ritualistic purposes. One guy wanted to affix crime scene photos to those O.J.-signed envelopes and offered me $250,000 for them. They are still in one of my storage units.

By the time I got to Rockingham it was dark, some time after 8:00 PM. The media mob had descended there, predictably, and engulfed the neighborhood. As far as the eye could see there were news vans, trucks, satellite dishes, and swarms of reporters from practically every country in the world. The house itself had been barraged with deliveries from friends, well-wishers and, we later learned, journalists trying to get inside. Flowers, telegrams, pizzas, ice cream, cakes—everything imaginable was delivered to the house. Before long, it was discovered that the tabloids had made floral deliveries and planted microphones inside the flowers. Other reporters ordered deliveries of various items to be made so they could try to sneak inside when the gates opened, or at least shout questions. Before long, all deliveries had to be left outside the front gate and examined by the security guards.

Those guards opened the gate for me and I went inside. I had only one thing on my mind—to see O.J. The first person I saw inside the house was Larry Schiller, who was there because he had exclusive rights with a tabloid for pictures of O.J. on the day of his acquittal. "Hey, you're late."

"I was working," I said. I spotted Cathy. She said O.J. was upstairs in his bedroom. The party was winding down by the time I got there, as it had been going on most of the day. I greeted a few people, and then quickly went up to the bedroom. The door was ajar. I knocked and walked in.

O.J. was lying on the bed propped up against some pillows. Gretchen Stockdale, whom O.J. later dated, was sitting on the edge of the bed, looking quite stunning. Gretchen testified in the trial about a voicemail O.J. left for her on the night of the murders. Because Gretchen was jaw-droppingly beautiful, prosecutor Marcia Clark probably assumed she would have the IQ of a raisin. But Gretchen got on the witness stand and dismantled Clark. Everybody on the defense team was blown away. Marcia kept trying to corner her and make her look stupid, but she just couldn't do it.

Gretchen graduated from law school a few years later. I was very happy for her when she broke up with O.J. (which she'd done after she found he was cheating on her). Of all the people I met through O.J., she and Skip Taft are my favorites. Gretchen was very different from some of the other beauties O.J. dated—like the one who told me, "I knew that I should be with O.J. because my birthmark looks like Africa." She did have a birthmark, and it did look like Africa, but what a thing to say.

This same girlfriend visited him in jail. She asked him, "O.J., do you remember when we went to that big dam in Buffalo?"

Big dam? I thought. In Buffalo?

O.J. and I looked at each other. At the same moment O.J. and I clicked and we both said, "Niagara Falls?"

"Yeah, that's it."

"That's a waterfall," I said, "not a dam."

"Well, I'm not good with geometry."

"Geography," O.J. said, "not geometry."

I later told O.J., "If you get out of here and you marry her, I'll kill *you*."

O.J. lit up when he saw me enter his bedroom. "*Michael Gilbert*!" he called out, and pulled me right onto the bed on top of him, hugging and kissing me.

"Hey, don't give me jail sex, man," I joked. "You're the one who's been in jail for a year and a half, not me."

He laughed, and I sat down on the bed. "I told you I'd see you at Rockingham," I said.

"You did, you certainly did. Where the fuck have you been all day, anyway?"

"Well, while you all were partying, I was working. Making sure we can keep paying all our bills around here." I showed him one of the envelopes and explained about the post office.

"I should have figured, knowing you."

Somebody brought me a glass of champagne. We all talked and bantered for probably two hours about the verdict and our reactions when it was read. People always ask me about O.J.'s own response to the verdict that night, and all I can remember is that he said he was extremely happy. I don't remember specifically what his words were. I do remember that at one point he looked around his bedroom and said, "This is so *good*, to be back in my own bedroom, in my own bed." He was euphoric.

Around midnight, I excused myself and told O.J. I would be back in the morning. He hugged me goodbye and thanked me again. I said goodbye to Gretchen and the others, left the party, and drove to my hotel, totally exhausted. As I lay on my hotel bed, I thought: "Wow. It's all over. It's done. The nightmare is finished. We can all get back to real life now. Everything is going to be normal again." I reflected on how much my world had changed in just twenty-four hours.

I flipped on the TV and immediately learned how wrong I was. Every station was covering it, talking about it. They were showing people's reactions. Almost every single person was not only negative but shocked, disgusted, and outraged. I flipped channels, but they were all the same, everywhere the same story, and within that story there was only one emotion: hate.

You may well call me naïve or worse for not having anticipated this, but I didn't. I remember O.J. in jail, talking very confidently about being on the A-list for every party in Hollywood if he were acquitted. We in the inner circle were an insulated society, with emotions, values, instincts, and reactions that weren't checked against the wider world; but after the acquittal, our bubble world was suddenly pressed against the real world, and for the first time I could see that we weren't even close to putting this nightmare behind us. I had a sick feeling: like having run a marathon, thinking you've almost made it, with your lungs and your heart about to burst, only to see the finish line receding farther and farther away. I went from pure jubilation, full of energy and hope, to desperation. *It's not over.* Not even close. It was like seeing thousands of raised pitchforks coming down over a hill straight toward your street. This was war, and it had only just begun.

The next morning I turned on the news to see if there was anything I could grasp for comfort. There wasn't. It was the same, on every channel, the same rage-filled responses. They were showing protesters outside Rockingham with signs that read: "Murderer," "Butcher," or, "Get Out of Our Neighborhood, Killer!" They showed a barricade near the house that somebody had spray-painted with the word "Murderer."

I thought to myself, I hope he's not seeing this shit. But of course, he was. He was watching TV just like everybody else.

A lot of the anti-O.J. sentiment at that time was being driven by feminist groups, particularly the National Organization for Women. Even I was a target. Tammy Bruce, then the head of NOW's Los Angeles chapter, recorded an outgoing message on NOW's answering machine not long after O.J.'s acquittal giving *my* home and cell numbers, urging people to call me and tell me what they thought of me. I fielded hundreds of calls—everybody from furious feminists to white supremacists. I decided to talk to as many of the callers as possible, rather than just hide. I engaged them in real discussions about what it means to respect the rights of others, and what it means to incite hate like Ms. Bruce had done. I recorded a few of the most hate-spewing messages I got, including some from racist groups, and gave them to CNN, which aired a segment on the calls. They confronted Tammy Bruce with a recording of her outgoing message. Her only quote was deeply sarcastic: "Well, welcome to the *real* world, Mike Gilbert." Tammy Bruce never made any attempt to speak with me.

Denise Brown, who had reinvented herself as an anti-domestic violence spokesperson, was being interviewed everywhere, furiously denouncing O.J. as a wife-beater and murderer. To the best of my knowledge, when Nicole was alive, nobody in her family had ever urged her to leave O.J.—not even after the 911 call. Her parents, without question, always urged her to stay in the marriage and try to hold it together. O.J. was very well-liked by Nicole's family as far as I could tell. He was practically Santa Claus. O.J. had once told me that he had paid for the college tuition of Nicole's sisters, Denise and Dominique, and had set Lou Brown up with the Hertz car dealership he ran. He frequently paid for the family to vacation in places like Hawaii. This was not lost on the black members of O.J.'s family. His sister Shirley used to comment that at Christmas, and other times, Nicole spent much more of O.J.'s money on what she called "the white folks."

There is an illuminating passage in Faye Resnick's book about the role Nicole's family played in all this mess. In the passage, Nicole has just revealed to Faye about the numerous beatings, detailing the one when O.J. beat her and locked her in a closet for hours.

> "Jesus, Nicole! What about your parents—and your sisters?... What kind of relationship do you have?" Nicole shrugged. "We used to be very close. But when I left O.J., they weren't at all supportive. They absolutely wanted me to stay with O.J. It's just like everything else, Faye. O.J. always controls everyone and everything around him.
>
> "Is that possible, Nicole? These are the people you grew up with."

"Faye, you just don't understand. O.J.'s done a lot for my family. They love him. I'm not saying they don't love me. They do. They're wonderful. They just love him more."

At the time, nobody was permitted the faintest hint of commentary on who O.J. Simpson was, or had been, other than "murderer." It seemed that all you had to do to be a public hero or heroine was denounce O.J. as a killer.

This outpouring of hate reinforced my wish to protect O.J. The attacks were so vicious I felt I had no choice but to fight back. My position was, in a sense, defined in opposition to theirs. If we could have talked like reasonable people, we would have found points of mutual agreement. I never said—ever—that I thought O.J. was not guilty of the murders. But I still wanted to defend other aspects of the truth about him. Prior to the murders, I'd known him to be a generous person and a good friend. I always used to quote a line of Richard Gere's from the movie *Primal Fear*. In that movie, Gere plays a criminal attorney who defends a killer in court. He is in a bar with a journalist who asks him why he does what he does, why he defends the guilty. He replies,

> I believe in the notion that people are innocent until proven guilty. I believe in that notion because I choose to believe in the basic goodness in people. I choose to believe that not all crimes are committed by bad people and try to understand that some very good people do some very bad things.

I got to Rockingham that morning with a knot in my stomach. I took something to eat out of the fridge and then went upstairs to O.J., who was still in bed. He muted the TV when I came in. He was furious after watching interviews with Denise and various hardcore feminists.

"Can you believe this shit? I was found fucking *not guilty*. This is bull-shit. These women would never have defended Nicole when she was alive. These are the same types of women who hated women like Nicole, and hated what she was. That she didn't have an education, that she married a rich guy, got by in life on her looks. Now they're gonna use Nicole for a membership drive? This is fucking crazy."

I saw the shirt and suit he'd been wearing the day before, when the ver-dict was read, crumpled on the floor near the closet. I picked it up and put it on a hanger.

Always thinking business, I asked, "O.J., what are you going to do with this? This is a piece of history now."

He looked over. "You want it? Take it. You can have it if you want it. That's the least I can do. Take it." And I did.

As I left that afternoon, I was struck by the noise of the media who had simply moved "Camp O.J." to surround his house and watch his every move. He couldn't go out. He had to stay in the house, for now, at all times. It occurred to me then that he had gone from being a prisoner in jail to being a prisoner in his house. The only difference was his cell was bigger now. And now he had something worse than chains. The guards at the jail had maintained strict order around him, and he had been sheltered from the reality outside, from the rage of the mob. This rage only matured fully when he was acquitted. Now he was on his own, and he found his world getting more and more ominous and claustrophobic. He was hunted, hated, exiled. Little by little, he lost everything that had ever mattered to him, beginning with his image, his friends, his business partners. Eventu-ally he lost his house, his possessions, even his Heisman trophy.

People ask me where the suit is today. It's still in my possession. It still has a fleck of blood on the collar of the shirt, where he cut himself shav-ing the morning he was released. I know the world of memorabilia col-lectors, and how much they are willing to spend to own an iconic piece of

American pop culture history. I've been offered as much as $50,000 for the suit. At one point, a representative of Howard Stern's declared that he wanted to buy it, in order to set it on fire in Times Square. I never participated in, or provided materials for, any of this kind of O.J. voodoo being acted out.

I never sold the suit, not even when I was dead broke. At least that's something small to be proud of.

CHAPTER ELEVEN

HE DID IT

O.J. and I were alone at Rockingham, with nobody around, a few weeks later. The kids were with their grandparents, the Browns, and the security guard was out in the guard shack. We had finished some business we had to tend to, and I was spending the night there and driving home to Hanford the next day. We had been upstairs, and O.J. had gone out on the balcony to smoke some pot, a habit he acquired after the criminal trial. Marijuana had the same effect on him that it has on most people: it made him slow, a little bit melancholy, and more relaxed. It was pouring rain outside, and that had a calming effect too (as did the Ambien he had just taken). We were both drinking beers, and for once we weren't trying to get anything done, or struggling to evade some immense impending threat.

It was a long, strangely hazy night. We sat around, we talked. Sometimes we sat quietly and said nothing. At one point it stopped raining, and O.J. took me outside because he wanted to show me something. It was a huge tree in the backyard that I had never given any particular thought to before.

He told me it had been a very special tree to both him and Nicole, but especially to Nicole. "Nicole loved this tree," he said. "It was dying and we got on a crusade to save it. Spent thousands, and consulted all these tree specialists. It took a lot of work but finally we turned it around." He showed me where they had carved their initials into the trunk. He liked to go stand under that tree, he said.

We made our way back into the house, and sat down in the living room. It started raining again and the only sound was the rain against the windows. O.J. sat solemnly, silent and introspective.

I had never wanted to ask O.J. about the murders. Part of me just didn't want to know. But that long, solemn night led me to give in to my deeper curiosity. I wanted to ask him about a conversation I had had with Al Cowlings, his best friend.

O.J. had always denied that he was involved with the murders, and his denials were always rooted in his claim that he had not even been at the scene of the crime. This was false, A.C. told me, indirectly at first, and then directly. First, A.C. had told a man named Mike Pullers that O.J. had confessed to being at the scene of the crime the night the murders took place—Pullers had passed this on to me. Then I asked A.C. about it directly. We were at the Hyatt hotel not long after O.J. was incarcerated, and he was signing black-and-white NFL photographs of himself and O.J.

"Mike Pullers told me, that you told him, that O.J. told you he went there that night but didn't bring a knife." A.C. came clean right away, and confirmed what I had heard from Mike Pullers.

"Yeah, he said he went over there, but that he didn't take a knife."

We knew he was guilty, and my own sense of guilt burst out.

"So then why is it okay?" I asked. "Why do we stay with him? Why do we continue to defend him?"

I remember A.C.'s words very clearly. He said, pretty forcefully, "What good would it do? Mike, it's like this. The kids already don't have a mom. If we help put O.J. in jail for the rest of his life, then they don't have a dad. Well, they'll have a dad, but he'll be in prison and they'll know that he murdered their mother. We can't do that to them."

I nodded. Part of me accepted this simple inner-circle logic. Another part of me felt something else, but I didn't say it. The something else was the obvious: We should tell what we know for the sake of justice.

Aside from not wanting to hurt his kids, there was another reason we stuck with O.J. We all knew that he wasn't a crazed killer, like a Charles Manson type. We knew that everything had aligned that night for this catastrophe to occur, and that it would never happen again. Everything that could go wrong that night did go wrong. Nicole had shunned him and none of the people whom O.J. would call when he needed to vent about Nicole were around. All of us were away. There was nobody there to reel him back in.

ı   ı   ı   ı   ı   ı

And so, as O.J. and I sat there, in the quiet stillness of the night, I decided to cut out the middleman. I wasn't satisfied with hearing a secondhand confession. Hearing A.C. say that O.J. went over to Nicole's on the night of the murders was one thing, but I wanted to hear it from O.J. himself.

It was now or never, I felt. This was my chance. I didn't know if I really wanted to know the answer, but something about the atmosphere that night gave me the courage to ask him. I remember trying to steady my voice.

"O.J.," I said, "what happened that night? What happened on June 12?"

He took a breath, and leaned back. He gave a familiar sigh. He got a very pensive look on his face. He looked at me. "What do *you* think?" he said. "What do you think happened that night, Mike?"

I hesitated for a while. I thought: do I just give him the same pat answer that everybody gives him? I gave very careful consideration to what I was about to say, and how I was going to say it. I finally answered: "O.J., I believe you were there. I have always believed you were there. In fact, the first thing I said when I heard the news was, 'So he finally did it.' Whatever happened . . . happened. I don't believe it was your intention. I don't know if *you* know you did it, if you think you did it, but yes, I believe that . . . you did it."

I remember looking at him as I was saying this, and waiting for shock, waiting for him to stop me. But he didn't. He looked at me with no expression, no emotion, nothing.

Then he said, "Mike, I did go there that night, but I didn't take a knife."

It was quiet for a moment and then I said gently, "I know that, because you told that to A.C."

O.J. showed no emotion. I pressed further.

"O.J., you told A.C. that Nicole opened the door with a knife in her hand."

"Yeah, I didn't take a knife over there. Nicole opened the door with a knife in *her* hand."

He sat quietly.

I waited. A few seconds passed, and then he continued, in a very soft and low mumble, almost as if he were sleep talking.

"If she hadn't opened that door with a knife in her hand, Mike, she'd still be alive."

We didn't say any more.

Nothing more needed to be said.

O.J. had confessed to me. There is no doubt in my mind whatsoever. The whole atmosphere of the room and the space between us changed.

There was a gravity and a silence, and also a sadness. There was something else as well. We weren't wearing our costumes, our masks. We were being real, for once—both of us.

We decided to turn in for the night. O.J. made his way up the spiral staircase to his room. He looked old and defeated. I remained downstairs. What had just happened started to hit me. I had asked to be burdened with the truth, and now I was. I felt very strange. I didn't know how to feel. It was so quiet in the house, and I was all alone with a man who had just confessed to murder. I went into the kitchen to get some fruit—a couple of apples—and a knife to cut them with. I brought the fruit and the knife with me to my room. In the eerie quiet, I started getting more and more apprehensive. I wanted to barricade the bedroom doors, but it was a double door that opened outward and it was impossible. I placed a chair and my suitcase near the door, and placed the knife on the bedside table, just as a neurotic form of imaginary protection. What if O.J. decided that he had said too much? I knew my mind was playing tricks on me and that I was being paranoid. I also wondered what I would do if O.J. knocked on my door. Would I open the door with a knife in *my* hand?

As I lay in that bed that night, I realized that the truth had been right in front of us the entire time.

"If she hadn't opened that door with a knife in her hand, Mike, she'd still be alive."

CHAPTER TWELVE

SELLING O.J. PIECE BY PIECE

The public hatred of O.J. after he was acquitted was like a twister always at our heels, wild and unpredictable. O.J. had a huge karmic bill to pay and he had walked out on it. Now our world of adoring crowds had turned into angry, indignant mobs. No matter where we went, people seemed to feel that O.J. had robbed them *personally* of something they were entitled to—whether it was a sense of justice or the illusion of him as a hero. As for me, I too became a public enemy for a time. Maybe not number one, but perhaps number two or three. Well, at least, I was on the list.

I can hear his voice on my answering machine to this day. Gruff and menacing: "Gilbert, you will be in the wrong place at the wrong time and I'll kill you *and* your nigger client. We'll kill your kids too, cut their throats like Ron and Nicole, and leave them on your doorstep."

Charming. And that was just one of the hundreds of calls I got after NOW's Tammy Bruce gave my number out to the world. I guess you could say they were wake-up calls. My golden goose of a client, my former idol whose name had been so adored, was now the most reviled man in the country.

I had to walk through the hate storm to believe it. Before it was all over, I would go from being pampered like a king, with five-star treatment wherever I went, to having my life threatened on a regular basis just for being O.J. Simpson's agent.

It was like something out of another century, or a bad movie, the levels of hate and terror that were unleashed by the O.J. verdict. Each day, we thought it would die down, and each day it just grew and grew.

I wish I had kept track and counted the number of times I had to hear the words "nigger" (about O.J.) and "white nigger" (about me). We were primarily targeted by two political groups when O.J. got out of jail: white supremacists and extreme feminists. Talk about your unholy alliances. I think everybody in between, "ordinary Americans," mostly got swept up in it, but would never have generated so much of an uproar if left to their own devices.

I got threats all the time from what I call "feminazis." Tammy Bruce's obsession with O.J. has been well documented. During the trial, she denounced O.J. with practically every breath she took on her L.A. talk radio show. When it was announced that a verdict was in she uncorked a bottle of champagne on air, she was so confident O.J. had been found guilty. When he was acquitted instead, she organized candlelight vigils and protest marches, leading thousands past his house in Rockingham.

In her crusading zeal, she made some huge and revealing tactical blunders. On ABC's *Nightline* she basically declared that abuse of women was a more important issue than racism, and actually blurted out that focusing on domestic violence provided "a needed break from all that talk of racism." Then she turned down an invitation to appear on a Philadelphia radio talk show, saying that she didn't want to "argue with a bunch of black women" about O.J.

Her superiors at NOW publicly censured her and apologized for those remarks. Bruce left NOW a few months later. She went on to become a popular would-be pundit on conservative media. Her Web site describes her as "an openly gay, pro-choice, gun owning, pro-death penalty, voted-for-President Bush authentic feminist."

I also got hate calls from the Klan, and from other white supremacist groups. "*You helped a nigger get away with murder. You are no better. You're a white nigger.*"

In the years I worked with O.J. after the trials, I witnessed all different kinds of reactions to him, ranging from adoring to near homicidal. It became part of my role as agent to deal with it and, if I could, to protect him.

One of the strangest nights of our immediate post-trial lives came in 1997, when I went with O.J. to a TV studio in Manhattan where Michael Moore, the filmmaker, was taping a pilot for a prospective FOX network talk show. Writer Celia Farber, on assignment from *Esquire,* was with us. Her 1998 article, "Whistling in the Dark," well captured the mood.

O.J. liked doing interviews, thinking he could convince people he was innocent, but they always left me nervous. The audience for this show was virtually all white and O.J. knew as well as anyone that while many blacks thought he was innocent, hardly any whites did. But the host, Michael Moore, had declared himself to be "the only white guy in America who thinks O.J. might not have done it," and O.J. expected a good reception.

He was a surprise guest to the audience, and when Moore announced him, it seemed as if people couldn't believe it. There were a few claps, a few nervous chuckles, and a few boos. Moore started with football questions, but the audience was obviously uneasy, and he shifted gears.

"So, did you kill her?"

"No."

"Did you kill her?" he repeated.

"No, I did not."

"Did you kill him?"

"Absolutely not."

The audience wasn't buying it. A woman shouted out, "Wife beater! You beat Nicole! You beat her! You know you did!"

Moore followed up on the woman's lead and got O.J. to admit: "We did get physical on one or two occasions. And I regret that. I do regret that."

"In other words, you beat her."

"Call it whatever you want."

Moore asked for a show of hands on how many people thought O.J. was guilty. The vast majority of the audience raised their hands, and with the hands came yells of "Murderer!" Moore finished the interview by asking O.J. whether he'd take an immediate lie detector test. I almost passed out. This whole thing was a disaster, in my opinion—and they'd never mentioned a lie detector test before. But this was Moore's idea of a joke.

But then, as usual, even though so much of the audience hated him, when the show was over, people ran up to get his picture and his autograph. That's part of what made it worthwhile for O.J.—it made him think that people still liked him after all.

Celia asked O.J., "What did Moore say to you after the show?"

"Oh, he said the audience had been a little rough. But I told him, 'No, you don't understand, this is what I want. I have always wanted this kind of dialogue.' I keep saying I'll go on any show and debate."

Celia and I departed the event in the same car. "Thank God that's over," I said in nervous exhaustion. O.J. might have enjoyed events like this, but for me they were torture. I felt every accusation, every look of hate, as a barb in my own flesh. Some people said I couldn't separate myself from O.J., and they were right, I couldn't. I took the whole thing personally. O.J., on the other hand, thrived on the interaction, the reassurance that people did still like him, and he was euphoric.

But neither one of us could ever get away from that sense of hate. O.J. had celebrated the night before at the bar in his hotel with some friends, including his new twenty-two-year-old girlfriend, Christie Prody. He was laughing and joking and telling stories, when suddenly a man came by and spat on the ground in front of him. Then a woman screamed at him, calling him a murderer. Celia witnessed all this and wrote:

> O.J. is a little quiet after that. This was personal, much more so than the hostile questioning from the TV audience. He is still smiling, but his mood is different—like a pane of glass that is shattered but still intact. It's a mood I've had glimpses of before, moments when he seems almost absent. I think about an eerie remark a friend of his made to me recently.
>
> "He still laughs the same," the friend said when I pressed him on how O.J. has changed since the murders, "He does the handshakes and the crowd pleasing, but he is . . . different. He's like a person who's had a mild stroke. He's not the same."

Despite these kinds of scenes occurring regularly, my phone still rang off the hook with people wanting to book O.J. for public appearances after his release. The very first post-jail deal we attempted was with a Pennsylvania-based company called Signature Rookies, a major sports card memorabilia company. The deal was an appearance and autograph contract for $1 million. O.J. had to make an appearance and sign about 50,000 autographs over the course of a year. We also agreed to give Signature Rookies the positive letters that O.J. received in jail, so they could market them to O.J.'s fans. O.J. had received hundreds of thousands of letters while he was in jail, and despite some hate mail, most of it was supportive. He received money, war medals, crosses, and thousands of Bibles. The gentlemen from Signature Rookies and I were to have a press conference in New York to announce the deal within a few days of O.J.'s release.

Meanwhile, O.J. was booked to do an unpaid interview with Bryant Gumbel of NBC four days after the verdict. O.J. believed this interview would take care of everything. He would explain his way out and be rehabilitated in the public mind.

The president of NBC West Coast, Don Ohlmeyer, a close friend of O.J.'s, called him and warned him that it was going to be "brutal," and that there was nothing he could do personally to help or protect O.J., because this was not his department. This was not NBC entertainment, but NBC news.

At that point, O.J. started to get worried, but he still wanted to do it. He wanted his image back, very badly. He was obsessed with doing what he imagined to be the great, Everything-Is-Forgiven TV interview, where he would be heard, understood, believed, and redeemed.

But the skies were darkening and the drums were beating. Now NBC was dealing with bomb threats, mass public outrage, and threats of boycotts.

O.J.'s attorneys, meanwhile, cautioned him that everything that came out of his mouth would be used against him in the pending civil suit—everything. They told him to watch every single word he said in private and public. Well, that's useless advice to a nonstop talker like O.J.

On the day of the scheduled NBC interview, I got a call from Skip. "Mike, O.J. canceled the interview. He's not going to do it."

We regrouped and talked about what to do next. Most of us thought this was a minor storm that would pass, and that maybe if we just lay low the tide would turn by itself in a few days. I was the one most in favor of putting O.J. back out there. I told O.J. and Skip that we needed to do something to turn public opinion, or at least spin public opinion.

"If we don't, we're just sitting here taking a beating," I said. "It's just going to get worse. We're sitting ducks."

I met with Signature Rookies and we all agreed to put the press conference on hold, sit back, and wait for the storm to pass. In the coming days and weeks, it just got worse and worse. Anti-O.J. sentiment had metastasized into a cult or crypto-religion within days of his release, and there was nothing anybody could say or do to affect it.

Soon we realized that anybody who did business with us would themselves be jeopardized—we're talking bomb threats, the need for beefed-up security, and buildings having to be evacuated because word got out that O.J. was going to make an appearance—and it came down to whether we could force them to honor their contracts. One guy we dealt with, who tried to make a deal with us for O.J. to appear in Atlantic City, put out a flyer with a picture of the white Bronco. This was after I'd warned him to focus the publicity on football. All holy hell broke loose: The casino was inundated with calls and received bomb threats, and the local police told the guy he'd have to fork over an extra $100,000 for security if O.J. were going to appear there. Finally he called me from his mother's house, quivering, and said he feared for his life. "Mike, I can't leave my house." Reporters had surrounded his own house, dug up the entire history of his life, and brought out dirty laundry he didn't want aired. He begged me to let him out of the contract, and finally we dissolved it.

Signature Rookies wound up asking me if they could form a secondary, front company just so their name would not be targeted for hate mail and protests. I feared that a second company, which had no assets, would just be a way for them to get out of the contract legally. And sure enough, after a few weeks, they were openly looking for ways to do just that. We eventually dissolved it. Signature Rookies went bankrupt a year or two later. I believe that it died of the O.J. plague, not natural causes.

There would be many, many more opportunities to market O.J. memorabilia, O.J.'s signature—O.J. himself—over the coming years. Almost everyone involved in the O.J. case, on both sides, marketed their experiences somehow. Everything had a price, and everybody was buying or selling. Those on the side of the victims were, in many cases, the ones who profited most. Prosecutor Marcia Clark got a $4.2 million advance for her book on the trial and pursued a post-O.J. career as a television expert on criminal justice. Mark Fuhrman's book became a number-one *New York Times* bestseller. Nicole Simpson's father sold her diaries to the *National Enquirer*,* the same paper to which her sister sold topless photos of Nicole. Nicole's parents profited from allowing O.J. and Nicole's wedding video to be used on *A Current Affair*.

As one L.A.-based TV correspondent who toiled long hours during the trials said, "I think he's guilty, but I bought my house because of this guy."

At the center of this industry stood O.J. himself—a pariah, at least in American public life, but still the possessor of a legendary autograph. Once it was a sports hero's signature, then it was an infamous one, but maybe also a historic one.

For years after the verdict, I arranged for O.J. to do a private signing for memorabilia dealers about once a month. It continued month after month, year in and year out. A typical signing would be in a hotel conference room where O.J. would sign hundreds of items—maybe two hundred footballs, one hundred USC jerseys, one hundred Buffalo Bills jerseys. He signed several thousand items a year.

Of course, O.J.'s finances and life went from complicated to surreal after the 1997 civil trial found him liable for the killings, and put a price tag of $33.5 million on his punitive debt. During the trial, the survivors of Nicole and Ron Goldman asserted that O.J. was worth at least $15.7 million. His financial advisers argued, to no avail, that he was actually $9 mil-

---

*He claimed she had left them in her safe deposit box in an envelope addressed "to Dad." But oddly enough, he could never produce the envelope.

lion in debt after paying for his criminal defense, and that his future earning prospects were minimal.

Even before the murders, O.J.'s net worth was estimated at no more than $10 million. Despite that, on March 9, 1997, a jury awarded the plaintiffs a total of $33.5 million in compensatory and punitive damages. Fred Goldman's share was worth almost $13.5 million. His ex-wife, Sharon Rufo, Ron's mother, had not seen her son for fourteen years and was accordingly awarded "only" $7.5 million. The estate of Nicole Brown Simpson, which included Sydney and Justin, was awarded $12.5 million.

The judgment was based on the faulty assumption by an expert witness during the trial,* who declared that O.J. Simpson would be able to earn around $3 million a year by telling his story and signing autographs. That was totally absurd. In my estimate, he could average at the most $75,000 to $100,000 a year doing autographs. I couldn't guarantee Michael Jordan $3 million a year for the rest of his life from signatures because at a certain point, the market becomes saturated. And as far as selling his story goes, one can only sell their story so many times.

Winning the civil judgment against him was one thing. Collecting it was another matter. In fact, the size of the award made it virtually impossible for the Brown or Goldman families to collect.

You see, to get the money from O.J., they would have to catch him as soon as he made the money and before he could spend it. The only money the Brown and Goldman families received was from auctioning off O.J.'s things. They also received money—about $8,000—from me. I had formed a company called Locker 32 that was mistakenly thought to be one of O.J.'s companies. My attorney advised me that I would spend more money defending my case than I would if I just turned over the income.

---

*I was supposed to testify for the defense about O.J.'s earning potential. Petrocelli objected. I was not allowed to testify because O.J.'s attorneys had not made me available to be deposed as an expert witness.

As the years rolled by, O.J. did not pay any of his mammoth debt, which I believe grew by almost $10,000 *a day* in interest alone. The Brown and Goldman families wanted to seize and auction not only O.J.'s most valuable possessions, but also the revered objects from his football career: things like his Heisman trophy, his NFL game-worn jerseys, and his original Buffalo Bills game-played footballs.

O.J., of course, was utterly defiant and uncooperative. It was a very strange situation, to say the least. He owed $33.5 million that he did not have to the families of a man and woman he had been found "not guilty" of killing in a criminal trial.

We knew, at a certain point, that we were going to lose everything. The funny thing is, we became adept at that too—at losing. We did it shrewdly.

We knew, for example, that we were going to lose the civil suit in Santa Monica almost as soon as it began, for the obvious reasons that Santa Monica is predominantly white and the burden of proof is much lower in a civil suit. Our focus was to keep the dollar amount of the judgment as low as possible.

O.J. had blown through astronomical sums of money during the criminal trial. Between lawyer's fees, expert fees, travel expenses, court fees, and so on, it was as much as $25,000 and probably never less than $10,000 a day. He started losing money from the moment he went to jail. He immediately lost all his endorsement deals. It never even had to be formally spoken; I just let those go without a word. What do you say?

"Oh, *really*, you don't want O.J. to be your spokesperson anymore? Gee, why not?"

O.J. lost most of his $10 million fortune in jail, paying for his defense. He was still paying off various lawyers long after he got out, sometimes with cars or other highly valuable objects, to settle debts.

I was with him in jail when he was served the papers for the first civil suit, filed by Sharon Rufo, Ron Goldman's birth mother. He was floored.

He said, "Looks like she's just getting in line first." Civil suits were always hovering on our minds as the next major crisis—but first we had to get O.J. out of jail.

When he did get out of jail, his fortune was pretty much gone. All he had in front of him at that point was his NFL pension (O.J. got a $25,000-a-month NFL pension that no civil judgment could touch), whatever money we could raise doing signings, and insanely, the monetary value of a true confession of the murders, if he decided to go that route. Once upon a time his money rolled in because of his work and investments. Now his only remaining worth was to confess to two brutal murders. If he did that, the assets would of course be owed to the civil judgment. (What Judith Regan was thinking when she decided to pay O.J. $3.5 million to write his confessional book, *If I Did It*, which he has since called "a fictional account," is anybody's guess.)

He also had many valuable possessions—cars, houses, condos, art, expensive carpets, lamps, and all kinds of sports memorabilia (mostly his own). Between legal debts for the two trials, the civil judgment, and the destruction of his name, he resigned himself to losing his earthly possessions, and in typical O.J. style, feigned disinterest. He had worked very hard to amass all this wealth, all these things, but once his image and status were destroyed, he no longer had the deep connection to it, or the need for it. At least, he pretended not to.

One thing that did infuriate him was when we got a notice from Fred Goldman's attorneys that they had found out that O.J.'s mother, Eunice, lived in a fairly valuable home that was in O.J.'s name. They went after that house while Eunice, age seventy-nine, was still in it. Eunice never got booted out of her house, but it was close.

Looking back, it seems like a biblical flood that carried away absolutely everything. I said to him once, when the financial cat and mouse game between O.J. and the Goldman team was well under way: "O.J., you are hurting yourself more than them. Instead of hiding from the Goldmans, why don't you make them a deal? Why don't we just end this thing? Go to Goldman and say, 'Listen, we'll give you 30 percent of whatever we generate.' It will stop all the rage, the protests—and we can say we are paying off the civil judgment. Our lives can be a little normal maybe."

"No," he said, darkly. "*Fuck* that. I am not going to give them a dime. They will get nothing."

"Okay, O.J., okay," I would say, with a sigh.

And so he lost and lost. The first condo he lost was the one he had in New York, on East 65th, in the Bristol Plaza. He lost another condo in Laguna Beach, and all the furniture was put into storage units in California. O.J. didn't want movers to move his things out of the New York condo, so he asked me if I would do it personally. I agreed, but told him it would cost more than movers would cost—renting a truck and driving across the country. He didn't care about the cost, he just didn't want movers to come in, mainly because he feared they would tip off the press.

"There's stuff in that apartment that belongs to my kids and that belonged to Nicole," he said. "I don't want people I don't know going through that stuff."

So my brother Larry and I flew to New York and rented a moving truck. It took us four days to pack it and three days to load it. Some of the stuff went to storage in California, some went to Rockingham, some went to Arnelle, O.J.'s oldest daughter. There was a wicker bedroom set in Sydney's room that O.J. told me Nicole had picked out. He wanted me to give it to my daughter Lindsay. She still has it.

We moved every last thing out during that week, and we managed to do it without the press finding out.

The next place we had to clear out was the Laguna Beach house he'd shared with Nicole. I took care of that house. I cleared that one out much faster—furniture, golf cart, household items, a jet ski. It was incredibly sad to walk around in that ghostly beach house. You could almost hear the shrieks of happy beach-bound kids, without a care in the world. I could see Nicole walking around barefoot, with a towel around her waist and her sunglasses up on her head, telling O.J. to shut up. Nicole was always barefoot when she could be.

We started selling off all the things that mattered least first, starting with the condo, a few cars—his Bentley and his Ferrari, the Laguna Beach house, his shares in restaurant chains—until we got down to the thing we all dreaded most.

The crown jewel of O.J.'s earthly possessions was Rockingham, the opulent, sprawling home he'd lived in since 1977.

Rockingham was a huge part of O.J.'s life. He had always loved that house more than just about anything. He'd lived there with both of his wives and raised two families there. He lived there through the best times of his life, and the worst. We never thought of it as "O.J.'s house." It was "Rockingham," just like Elvis's house was Graceland.

We knew they were going to place liens on O.J.'s property and possessions, but we did not know when or how. I arrived at Rockingham one day in 1997, with my son Luke, for what I thought was going to be a normal business day with O.J. Instead, when I pulled up I noticed several other cars, which was odd that early in the morning. I rolled into the driveway. People were taping up boxes and moving them out. I walked in and it was a madhouse, with all kinds of people walking around with cardboard boxes.

The first person I saw in the kitchen was Cathy Randa.

"Cathy, what's going on?"

"One of the guards at the L.A. jail sent us a fax, tipping us off that the sheriff is coming tomorrow morning to seize all of O.J.'s valuables. Anything we don't want them to seize we have to get out of here now." The

Goldmans had hired a moving company to come the next morning to pick up O.J.'s stuff.

O.J. was out playing golf. That way he had deniability; he wasn't involved. Everyone else was moving out his valuables like a moving company in high speed.

I took off my jacket and rolled up my sleeves. We had very little time, and it was just chaos: boxes, people, and things going this way and that. People took stuff to their homes, to storage, you name it. The problem was no one kept track of what went where.

The court order stated that O.J. was allowed to keep necessary living items, which created a gray area. A lamp is a necessity, but is a $65,000 Tiffany lamp a necessity? We found the Goldmans had obtained a list from O.J.'s insurance company, stating the value of every Persian carpet, Tiffany lamp, or other valuable object in the house. So the game plan was to move as much as we could, hide as much as we could, and replace that which could be replaced.

His good golf clubs, for example—I packed them into one of the cars. Then I went by the Salvation Army and bought some cheap old golf clubs and left them in the garage.

One of O.J.'s most prized possessions was his old USC jersey. It hung in a glass case in the living room. We couldn't let them seize that. We had a bunch of replica jerseys he would sign so we could sell them to the public. In fact, we found some in the house that he had mis-signed somehow. He might have misspelled a name, or the ink ran out. We decided to replace the real one with one of those. But the replica looked too new. So Benny, O.J.'s brother-in-law, and I had a great idea: we took it outside and rubbed it around on the lawn, kicked some dirt on it to make it look worn. That made us crack up, despite the stress of that day. We took apart the glass case and put the new dirty replica in there. "You'd never know," I said looking at it proudly.

We did the same with his authentic game balls, switched them for replicas. Virtually everything valuable that could be replaced was. It went on all night. At some point in the night O.J. wanted to come home. He'd played golf, he'd had some drinks afterward, and he was drunk and sleepy. But we weren't done and he couldn't see what we were doing. Also, if the sheriff knew he was home, he could serve O.J. the papers as of 12:01 AM, and we didn't want that, because we were nowhere near finished making all the replacements. So we had someone drive down the street, pick him up, and sneak him back into the house. O.J. crawled out of the backseat of the car and went inside the house through the garage. He was drunk, mumbling, stumbling, singing and whistling "If I Only Had a Brain" from *The Wizard of Oz*. He always used to sing or whistle that song.

"O.J., *shut up*," I said. "Nobody can know that you're here."

We packed him off to bed, while the rest of us went on taping boxes, loading cars, and driving around to various drop-off places for the rest of the night.

By 7:00 AM the only ones left in the house were my son Luke, asleep in Kato Kaelin's old room, O.J. asleep up in his room, and me. I was still loading items into my BMW, which looked like a low-rider because it was so loaded with stuff. I went up to O.J.'s bedroom to wake him, and saw the Goldmans' two moving trucks pulling up.

"I can't keep my eyes open," I told O.J. "We've done a lot, but there's stuff in the garage we couldn't get to. Take a real quick look before they come in."

We went downstairs and did a quick walk-through together. He was very impressed by how much we'd replaced. But he did point to a Persian rug and say, "No, no, we've got to grab this. Mike, you don't know how much this carpet is worth."

I rolled it up.

"O.J., I have to get out of here *now*. My car is on your property and they might want to go through it and see if I'm removing anything."

We went and woke Luke. O.J. ruffled his hair fondly, which he often did. We told Luke to get ready, and O.J. went upstairs. From his bedroom he shouted, "*Shit*. I can't have this around." I ran upstairs to see what was the problem.

He reached under his bed and pulled out this wicked-looking machine gun, some sort of fully automatic assault weapon. My eyes bugged.

"Where did *that* come from?"

"Oh, some guy over at SWAT."

Great scene, I was thinking. The sheriff, the Goldman movers, and the media knock on the door, and O.J. answers with a fully automatic assault weapon in his hand.

"We've got to hide it," I hissed.

So we dashed back downstairs. O.J. unrolled the Persian rug and rolled the gun up in it, and handed the bundle to me.

Then he walked me and Luke to the door and gave me a hug.

"Alright, buddy. Thanks for everything. I appreciate it. Luke, I'll see you later. Go get some breakfast."

I put the carpet with the gun in my trunk (somehow I made room). As I drove my low-rider BMW out the Rockingham gate, the sheriff and his crew were driving in the Ashford gate. As we drove away, Luke looked around the car sleepily and asked, "What's all this stuff, Dad?"

"It's just stuff we're keeping for Uncle O.J."

I kept expecting to see flashing lights in the mirror. I didn't relax until we reached the 405. We drove to a Denny's for breakfast.

That replica USC jersey was later sold for several thousand dollars by the Los Angeles auction house Butterfield and Butterfield in 1999, where many of O.J.'s valuables were auctioned off toward the civil judgment. The buyer took it to the courthouse of O.J.'s murder trial and burned it on the steps as a form of protest. Little did he know it was a cheap knock-off, made of polyester. Instead of just burning, the way the real 1960s, cotton-wool jersey would have, it almost exploded in his face. That should have tipped someone off that it was a fake, but it didn't.

And where is the real jersey? All I can tell you is that it is in a very safe and secure place.

Among the numerous other items auctioned off in 1999 was O.J.'s Heisman trophy. It went for $230,000. And it was the real one, not a fake.

I think ultimately I was much more emotionally attached to that thing than he was. To me, after all that had happened, the Heisman was the symbol of a paradise lost, a sacred object. It was a great achievement, a trophy he had won fair and square, and I fought long and hard to keep it from becoming a token of destruction, a way for people to vent their fury against O.J.

Fred Goldman had told the press that he wanted to get hold of the trophy so he could smash it with a sledgehammer. There was also talk of melting it down and making Nicole Brown Simpson angel pins out of it.

I wanted to do something—*anything*—to preserve that small piece of history, that memory of who O.J. had been, from the fury of the mob. It was very personal.

O.J. won that trophy the day his first child, Arnelle, was born, on December 4, 1968. My feeling was: they can punish him however they like, but they can't take this away. They can't take away what he did on the field.

Wrong again.

The battle over the Heisman was like the battle over O.J.'s soul. I wanted it protected at all costs because it symbolized O.J.'s achievements as an *athlete*. The Goldmans wanted it for that very same reason—to be able to achieve revenge on "O.J. Simpson" by crushing the very place where that identity was formed. Their objective, I believe, was to find a way to hurt O.J., which I must say he provoked by always taunting the Goldmans. For my part, I was no longer sure if I was defending O.J. Simpson the athlete,

O.J. Simpson the man, a vanquished dream, or my own self-image. All I knew was I had to fight.

In 1997, O.J. was ordered to turn over the Heisman along with other valuables as part of the civil judgment. Strangely enough, though, it had vanished from its glass case at Rockingham. O.J. testified in his deposition for the civil trial that he came home from golf one day and it was just not there. Like a missing Pepsi from the fridge or something. He was completely nonchalant about it and said he had no idea where it was. He claimed he didn't "really think much about it."

Fred Goldman's attorneys came after me and Skip Taft and accused us of hiding it, which we had not done. The Heisman was, at that time, being held by an attorney in L.A. who never worked on any of O.J.'s legal cases, but was a friend of O.J.'s. He also had lots of things that had been gathered by O.J.'s sister after we lost the judgment but before they collected on it. He kept these things safe in his condo, and nobody ever thought to look there.

We needed to turn it over, but the attorney would have been disbarred if it became known that he was hiding stuff for O.J. I agreed to fall on the sword. Our lie was that I had taken it and that O.J. had no idea I had done so. Of course, I didn't have it, and O.J. knew exactly where it was. We all just did what needed to get done, quietly, wink-wink, often without saying a word to any of the others, because it did not need to be said and one was careful not to rope in others when it could be avoided.

We knew we were going to have to turn it over, or some of us were going to wind up in jail, in contempt of court. I was given a deadline of December 15, 1997, to turn it over or go to jail. Finally we decided I would get the trophy from the attorney and turn it over to Ron Slate, one of O.J.'s attorneys, who would give it up. As a final act of defiance, before we walked into to Ron Slate's office, I had the sudden inspiration of removing the nameplate from the Heisman Trophy. I put it in my pocket along with the nails.

This was crazy of course, but I was stalling for time. If they didn't have the nameplate, in my mind, there was still a small piece of him, of O.J. the football hero, that they did not have. They could smash the trophy, burn it, melt it down, but this way, without the nameplate, they couldn't completely humiliate him. Because he won it on the day that Arnelle was born, I had always hoped Arnelle would get to keep it, and I felt that would have been fair. When I removed the nameplate, my thought was that maybe we could have another trophy made, and put O.J.'s nameplate on that one.

They had the trophy, but I had the nameplate *and* an idea. Why not create another O.J. Simpson Heisman trophy; a fraud? This would confuse potential buyers and lower O.J.'s financial liability (you see, O.J. said he had to pay taxes on the "income" he earned from his possessions being auctioned, so the less it sold for, the less he had to pay).

In December of that year I went, as I always do, to the Heisman annual meeting at the Downtown Athletic Club in New York. I asked a buddy of mine who was on the board for the Heisman if he could go to the executive office and bring up one of the extra Heisman trophies. They had a couple of extra ones that had been slightly damaged.

I nailed O.J.'s nameplate onto it, then took pictures of the trophy next to a copy of that day's *New York Times*, giving the perfect illusion that the "real" O.J. Simpson Heisman trophy was still on the loose, and that the one the sheriff's department had in its possession was a fake. We then sold those photos to a tabloid (for a handsome price) just before the real trophy was auctioned off. People were worried that the real trophy was a fake, and so it didn't sell at auction for nearly as much as people had initially thought. The operation was a success.

I never dreamed it would cause such a hell storm. Over the next several months, I was subpoenaed, deposed, and ordered by courts six different ways till sundown to turn over the nameplate or go to jail. I finally took it over to O.J., who had by then moved out of Rockingham to a house on Alta Mura.

I said, "O.J., it's up to you. You want me to hold it? I'll hold it, and go to jail."

O.J. was quiet for a moment, and then said, "Turn it over."

I handed it to O.J. He was holding it, looking at it. Then he got up, walked to a kitchen drawer, and took something out. At first I wasn't sure what he was doing. I walked over to him. He had a knife, and he was defacing the nameplate on the kitchen table.

I said, "O.J., stop. What are you doing? We can fight this. We'll get it back in court."

He said, "No, Mike, I'll never see it again."

"You can't be sure."

"Mike, we'll never see it again."

He started gashing the plate. The scratches weren't going deep enough. He grabbed a screwdriver and started digging with the screwdriver, slashing harder. This was *his* last act of defiance. But he was defacing himself.

I want to say to whomever owns the trophy (and the nameplate) today—if the person wants to know how all those scratches and gashes got there, it was done by O.J. There you have it.

By the way, I still have the original nails. I ran up more than $20,000 in legal bills over the Heisman and the nameplate. The guy who bought the trophy at the auction called me two times asking about those nails. I'm not giving them over.

When O.J. was questioned about it by *Rolling Stone* in 2000, he said, "I couldn't understand why anybody would want to buy somebody else's trophy. That was kind of perplexing. But losing the trophy really didn't mean that much to me. I guess I kind of wish I had it now, for my kids. I feel about football the way I feel about high school. It's part of my past. It's just something I did."

As usual, O.J. doesn't care, right? That's always his answer and his central lie, that he didn't care so much. Not about Nicole, not about her affair with Marcus, not about that trophy, not about what people think of him.

Of course he cares. He cares deeply. Why can't he be honest? This entire nightmare we have all been trapped in for almost fifteen years is the result of O.J.'s total inability to be honest. This, in turn, is a by-product of the culture of sports, hero worship, and celebrity. I, too, fostered and fed it— that was my profession as a sports marketing agent. It's a tissue of lies and delusions that we all create in order not to have to deal with the pain, humiliation, and difficulty of being real people, real men, who hurt, and cry, and suffer. None of that is tolerated or admitted in the narrow world of sports hero worship. If it were, the dream would fall apart.

Financially, the whole civil judgment was so bizarre and complex. The three parties had a joint settlement—the Browns, the Goldmans, and Sharon Rufo, Ron's mother. It wasn't divided equally three ways. It was very convoluted, based on who had spent what on lawyers and all kinds of factors, where human loss is calculated. Human loss, of course, is incalculable. In the end, it degenerated into what I call cannibalism, because instead of it being fair and equitable it became all about who got there first. O.J. was willing to let assets go to the estate of Nicole, (which meant his kids), but not to the Goldmans or Sharon Rufo. The Brown family, in turn, was left in a position where if they helped the Goldmans, they hurt Sydney and Justin. It was so Byzantine; I doubt anybody alive can describe it all accurately.

That 1999 auction reportedly netted the victims' families just under $400,000. Obviously, that didn't even make a dent in the interest on the $33.5 million O.J. was ordered to pay. If the judgment against O.J. had been for a few million dollars, we could have paid it off. Somebody could have paid it for him, possibly one of his wealthy friends. Instead, the enormous sum made it crushing, impossible, and even absurd.

At one point there was talk between the attorneys of a settlement, but the Goldmans rejected it. Maybe the Goldmans are telling the truth when they say "it's not about the money." What they want is to pursue O.J. to the last breath he draws. And I think they will.

I can't say I blame them.

I do, sincerely, empathize with the Goldmans. All those years, we all had what we called the "bunker mentality," and for me, the Goldmans were the bad guys, because of this battle we were in. But the longer I have been away from O.J. the worse I feel for Mr. Goldman. I wish I could take back every hurtful thing I ever said about him.

I put my sons' faces on Ron Goldman, and it breaks my heart. When I reviewed the timeline of June 12 as I was writing this book, I saw that he had clocked out of work at Mezzaluna at 9:33 PM, and apparently forty-two minutes later he was dead. Why? Because he was being a good guy, being thoughtful, being a good friend. He was doing the kind of thing my kids would do, returning somebody's glasses.

When I saw that timeline, I started thinking about what I was doing at that exact time, and I was really bothered. I was with my second son, David, enjoying Yosemite while Ron and Nicole were dying. It all hit me, hard, after all these years of extreme defensiveness. How often does Kim Goldman wish she could call her brother and she can't? How often does Fred Goldman imagine what Ron's life would have been like, or how many kids he might have had if he'd been allowed to live? And why? Because of O.J.

The Goldmans are the people I would most like to forgive me.

CHAPTER THIRTEEN

A BRIEF INTERLUDE: O.J.'S LIES SIMPLIFIED

I don't think many people ever believed that O.J. was, as he put it, "absolutely, positively 100 percent not guilty." I think most people who followed O.J.'s trial came away concluding that he was guilty. Even many of the black Americans who rejoiced on the day of his acquittal probably knew that he was guilty. They weren't rejoicing because they thought an innocent black man had been set free. They were just happy to see a black man and hero put one over on the Los Angeles legal system.

Anyone who cares to review what O.J. said back then (for instance, in the records of his police interrogation the day after the murders) and has said since (in the 2007 book *If I Did It*) can find a laundry list of vague, contradictory, suspicious, and categorically untrue statements. As someone intimately involved, I've got my own list. Here it is.

O.J. was a smart, charismatic, charming American hero. Naturally, he always felt that he could talk and charm his way out of anything—including murder, apparently. Although people warned him not to speak to the police after the murders, he went to the LAPD's Parker Center the next day, June 13, to be interrogated by detectives Phil Vannatter and Tom Lange. Reading the transcript, you can see O.J. losing confidence, becoming more frustrated and caught up in his own evasions as the interrogation proceeds.

In my opinion, they should have arrested him on the spot. Instead, they let him walk, only to arrange for him to give himself up a few days later (June 17, the white Bronco day). Mark Fuhrman later told me that if he and his partner had done the interrogation, O.J. would not have walked out of the jail that day.

Of course, the Dream Team later aided and abetted O.J. in his lies, evasions, and even preposterous claims:

- When O.J. was asked how he got the injury on his hand, he stated, "I don't know. The first time when I was in Chicago and all, in the house I was just running around." Vannatter followed up, "How did you do it in Chicago?"

- O.J. replied, "I broke a glass. One of you guys had just called me and I was in the bathroom and I just went bonkers for a bit."

  Tom Lange then asked, "Is that how you cut it?"

  At this point O.J. began changing his story. His mind was probably racing—*Why are they pressing me about this? Did they find blood at my house?*

  "It was cut before," he now said. "I think I opened it up again but I am not sure."

  Later still, O.J. suddenly recalled bleeding at Rockingham. "Yeah, I knew I was bleeding, I mean, it was no big deal. I bleed all the time. I play golf and stuff so there was always something, nicks here and there."

I've played golf for years, and I've never cut myself golfing.

O.J. flip-flopped several times over whether he had a bandage on or off, and where and when he put the bandage on.

It's worth noting that police had photographed and taken samples of the "trail of blood" leading away from the crime scene *before* O.J. came back from Chicago with his bloody knuckle. That is, the officers had no idea that O.J. had a cut on his finger until they saw him the next day at Parker Center.

• The blood found at the crime scene was later shown to contain O.J.'s DNA. O.J. said that he hadn't been at Nicole's house for a couple of weeks. So how did O.J.'s blood drops get there? O.J. offered no explanation.

• The bloody footprints walking away from the crime scene were made by Bruno Magli shoes that O.J. said that he never wore or owned. O.J. stated, "I would never wear those ugly-ass shoes."

Photographs of O.J. wearing the shoes later surfaced during the civil suit.

• Drops of blood were found in the Bronco—on the steering wheel, the instrument panel, the driver's door. A bloody shoe print, made by the same Bruno Magli shoes as at the crime scene, was on the carpet of the car.

O.J. stated that he may have cut himself and bled in the Bronco when he was reaching to get his cell phone.

That's possible. O.J. could have bled a week before the murders, or a day before.

What O.J. never explained away was how some of the blood in the Bronco tested as *Ronald Goldman's and Nicole's*. What, did all three of them go for a joyride together and cut themselves reaching for their cell phones?

• O.J. said that he allowed other people to drive the Bronco. He said that perhaps Kato Kaelin might have driven it.

To the best of my knowledge, O.J. *never* allowed Kato to drive his Bronco, ever.

• Witnesses testified that O.J. was in a dark and brooding mood at Sydney's dance recital on the day of the murders. O.J. denied it. The defense showed a video taken right after the recital of O.J. shaking hands with and smiling with his father-in-law, Lou Brown, and picking up Justin and giving him a kiss. The defense said, "Look at O.J. He's happy. He's smiling. Does this look like someone who is angry, upset, or brooding?"

O.J. later said to me about the video, "Mike, do I look like somebody pissed off, like I am about to kill my ex-wife? I'm smiling. I'm happy. Life is good."

I said, "If I can play the devil's advocate, I'd say the video means nothing. O.J., how often are people arguing with their wives or girlfriends, and then the phone rings or someone knocks at the door and they put on their public face? '*Hey*! How are you?'"

I reminded him of a time we were at the Radisson hotel in Buffalo, and he explained to me how he had to keep that happy public face and image around fans, no matter what his real mood was, because he only had one chance with them. "Mike, *you* can see me pissed off," he'd said that day, "but when a fan walks up they can't see that. They can only see me smile."

I'd seen O.J. turn on that smile many times. I can easily see him doing it at Sydney's recital, not letting Nicole or the Brown family or his kids see how angry and hurt he was.

• Then there were the Colombian drug lords to whom Faye Resnick supposedly owed money. That was one of the smelliest red herrings Johnnie Cochran tossed in front of the jury—that these mysterious drug lords had gone to Nicole's place looking for Faye, and ended up murdering Nicole and Ron.

We never offered anything like real evidence. It was all just more smoke and mirrors, innuendo and suggestion, at which Johnnie was a genius, and which the hapless Judge Ito allowed to an outrageous degree. Johnnie kept hounding Detective Tom Lange on the witness stand, demanding to know why the LAPD did not follow up on this Colombian drug cartel angle. Lange kept saying, because it wasn't an angle. And Johnnie was like, Oh *really*? Or could it be that you ignored this angle because it might prove O.J. innocent? The press corps rolled their eyes, but you could see the jury sitting there thinking "hmmmm...."

- O.J. stated that he never hit Nicole. He said that *she* would try to hit *him*, and he would defend himself.

There were incidents where, for instance, O.J. shattered Nicole's car windows. He would say, "It's not a crime. I paid for that car. I can do whatever the fuck I want to it." True enough. Ironically enough, Mark Fuhrman was the officer who came to the house to respond to the domestic dispute call.

There are photographs of a black-and-blue Nicole after O.J. beat her. Al Cowlings once took Nicole to the hospital, and was upset with O.J. for beating her to the point where she had a concussion. O.J. always denied punching Nicole, but he would say he did "wrestle" her, which is how she got her cuts and bruises.

He took off one night when the police were coming to talk to him about it. O.J. left the estate and later parked around the corner. He reentered the estate by walking along the fence line between his house and his neighbors'. He reentered the house, in other words, *exactly as he tried to reenter the house the night of the murders.* My contention is this: It was a repeated pattern. After he killed Nicole and Ron, he came home by an entrance he had used before when he was avoiding the police. This is why Allan Park, ringing the bell at the gate, didn't see him. This is why he dropped the bloody glove behind that wall.

When Mark Fuhrman questioned Kato, Kato said that he had heard a thump outside his room. If Kato had never said that, Fuhrman would never have gone to look behind the wall and find the glove. He was being a diligent cop. The evidence he collected should have convicted O.J. In my opinion, it was the mishandling of that evidence by Vannatter, Lange, and Marcia Clark—not Fuhrman's alleged use of the N-word—that got O.J. off the hook. O.J.'s claim that Mark Fuhrman was a racist cop who planted evidence is preposterous. If we are to believe O.J., Fuhrman was going to risk his career, retirement, and freedom in order to frame O.J.—all without knowing whether or not O.J. had an alibi.

• O.J. took a lie detector test, the results of which were not released to the public. He didn't just fail the test—he failed it with about the worst possible score you could get. He failed it miserably.

 When Lange asked O.J. what his thoughts were about taking the test, O.J. said, "Should I talk about my thoughts on that? I am sure eventually I will do it, but it's like I have got some weird thoughts now. I have had weird thoughts. . . . You know when you have been with a person for seventeen years you think everything. I've got to understand what this thing is . . . if it's true blue, I don't mind doing it."

 Among the "weird thoughts" O.J. was having about Nicole was a dream he told his friend Ron Shipp about: he said he'd dreamed about killing Nicole. No wonder he was hesitant about the test.

 After O.J.'s acquittal, when he wasn't welcomed back into society, I challenged him to take another lie detector test. O.J. said he would do it, but only for a million dollars.

 I said, "O.J., it's not about the money. It should be about public perception. If you take a lie detector test and pass you might be able to convince some people that you are innocent. It might go a long way. If you're so fucking innocent, do it. Take the lie detector test for free and prove your innocence. Do it. It would probably give your kids and all the people who supported you some peace of mind."

O.J. declined.

• At 10:03 PM on the night of the murders, O.J. alleges in his book *If I Did It* that a man named Charlie, whom he had met a few months earlier, told O.J. that some guys he knew had partied with Nicole and Faye a few months earlier in Cabo San Lucas. Charlie allegedly said that there were a lot of drugs and partying and things got pretty kinky.

O.J. says he and Charlie headed for Nicole's house with the idea of "scaring the shit out of Nicole." Charlie begged him not to go, but O.J. said he'd be quick since he had a flight to Chicago. They drove to Bundy and parked behind her condo. O.J. put on a knit cap and gloves so Nicole wouldn't recognize him when she came to the door.

Who is this Charlie? Why has he never come forward? He is the bearer of the world mass-media golden lottery ticket of the century, after all, having witnessed this, and he could cash in his millions if he stepped forward to corroborate O.J.'s story. Why would somebody who has only known O.J. for a few months become the most hardcore ally he ever had, keeping his silence all these years? There is no Charlie. But what purpose does he serve in O.J.'s imagination?

• In *If I Did It*, O.J. says that when they got to Nicole's, he heard music and knew she was expecting a visitor. Then some guy walks up, acting "like he owned the fucking place." O.J. demands, "Who the fuck are you?" It was Ron Goldman, coming to drop off Nicole's mother's glasses.

O.J. has always said he was through with Nicole by this point. It was over, done. He was moving on in his life. Why would he be so jealous to see Ron Goldman going over to her place? Why was he planning to do something so risky as to disguise himself and bring a knife to her place to "scare" her as some kind of bizarre prank, because some guy he didn't know well, this Charlie character, told him she'd been partying in Cabo?

O.J. claims he removed his right glove and grabbed the knife from Charlie. Then he goes into a blackout. "I remember how I got there, why I was there. But blacked out. The next thing I knew I had blood all over my shirt." (It is important to mention, I think, that O.J.'s "confession" in his book differs from the confession he made to me. He never mentioned a "Charlie" to me, and he explicitly stated that he did not take a knife with him over to Nicole's place.) And why did he feel the need to take off his glove to take the knife?

• About that knit cap and gloves: This was the middle of June, in Los Angeles. Why did O.J. have a knit cap and gloves at hand? What kind of fool would think that walking around in a knit cap and gloves in L.A. in June would *not* look suspicious and conspicuous?

About the disguise: O.J. said he had the disguise handy because he was planning on taking his kids to

Knott's Berry Farm and didn't want to be recognized and bothered by the public. All of us who have known O.J. have never known him to wear a disguise. He loved being famous and being recognized.

• When Allan Park was loading O.J. into the airport limo, Park handled all of O.J.'s bags except for one black bag, of which O.J. said, "No, I'll get that," in a very firm voice. He kept that bag in the back of the limo with him. Park saw him fiddling with it the entire ride. Both Kato and Allan Park remember the black bag in O.J.'s possession.

That bag did not come back from Chicago with O.J. To this day that bag has never been seen again.

• Within twenty-four to forty-eight hours of his ex-wife being murdered, O.J. was on the phone with his hotel in Chicago making sure that his golf bag was sent to him in California. At a time like that, when the mother of your kids has just been murdered, are you going to be concerned with a golf bag? When the bag arrived at LAX, Al Cowlings said he'd go pick it up. O.J. said firmly, *no*, he would go *alone*. Al gave him a ride to the airport. So within hours of his ex-wife's murder, O.J. goes to the airport to pick this thing up. When they pull up to the terminal, O.J. went alone to the baggage claim.

What was this all about? My belief is that O.J. had to make sure that nothing suspect was in that bag.

CHAPTER FOURTEEN

GOODBYE
TO ALL THAT

It was the last day at Rockingham. O.J. had lived in that house for almost twenty-one years. It had been his port in the storm and the one thing in his life that held its center, the one thing that didn't, in his mind, let him down or abandon or betray him. The house. You remember how badly he wanted to get to Rockingham both during the Bronco chase and when he got out of jail? "I want to go home," he said adamantly in both cases.

Nicole had also developed an acute longing for that house, not necessarily as the house she loved the most—that would have been her condo at Bundy—but as the house where life with O.J. was. She knew that to get back together with O.J. she had to get back into Rockingham. She pleaded with him to let her move back in. He was rather cold about it, refusing her each time. He was willing to start "dating" her again in that last year to see if it would work out, but he would not let her and the kids back into "his" house. I always found this relationship—between O.J. and his house—a little strange.

So the day had finally come. The house was virtually empty but for a few stray boxes, some broken lamps, things nobody wanted. All we had to do now was say goodbye and leave.

O.J. always flew the American flag in the front yard. I went out and looked at it, and felt an immense, complex sadness. We had come so close to living the American dream, actually holding it in our hands and knowing what it was. Now we were shipwrecked, packing up, and leaving, in disgrace, and also in confusion. What was it, really, exactly, that had caused our terrible downfall?

Double murder, you might say.

Fair enough.

But what caused those double murders?

O.J. Simpson, in a rage, with a knife.

Fair enough, but how did he get there, with that knife in hand, in that dark walkway, and why, when he had climbed so high, transcended so much, did he make a mistake that would cost him all of it in a few seconds of slashing fury?

This is the mystery.

I had a still camera and a video camera with me that last day at Rockingham. I documented everything. I filmed him taking down the flag for the last time. Then we walked through the house, room to room.

The house was empty. It creaked and echoed as we walked around. It was quite eerie. I wasn't the only person there—Cathy and a few others were there, as were my wife and our kids. I stayed close to O.J., while the others stayed busy with last-minute packing.

I tried to imagine what that must have felt like for him. What a punishment, I thought, as I watched him go from room to room. What was he seeing? What was he thinking?

Rockingham had been like headquarters for all of us. It had always been a warm, raucous place, always bursting with life, people, parties, food. O.J. and Nicole got married there. Marcus and Kathryn got married there. There were constant gatherings and parties at Rockingham. It was the house of good times. No, *great* times.

As I walked through, I had sensory hallucinations—the smell of turkey and baked ham, Thanksgiving and Christmas, the sound of squealing kids running all over, and maids and cooks everywhere. I thought I could hear Nicole's voice, calling to the kids, and O.J.'s booming voice, telling a joke or a story. I wondered: weren't we happy? Weren't we *normal*? Was there a malevolent thread lying in wait the whole time, waiting for circumstances to have it yanked, everything blown to bits?

You have to realize that we were an entire community that perished. The horror of it all, the shame, the guilt, the recriminations—that has silently, like a cancer, killed off everything, even our memories, the memory that we ever existed, or how we once felt about one another.

O.J. and I just walked around, not talking much.

When we got to O.J.'s office, he became very solemn. He was staring at the floor. He pointed to a part of the carpeted floor and said, "Right there . . . was the first place I ever made love to Nicole in this house. Right there."

He just stood there staring.

"O.J.," I said, "why don't you take part of the carpet? It's obviously very important to you."

"I can't destroy the carpet, Mike."

"Why not?" I said. "This means a lot to you. We don't have to take it out of the main floor, we can take a piece out of the closet."

I opened the door to a small closet in the office and got down on my knees with a box cutter in hand.

"I'm sure when they auction off the house they won't notice this."

I cut out two pieces. I gave one to him and, always the collector, kept one for myself.

You could see the traces of where photos had been hanging on the walls, now empty. O.J. always kept so many photos all over the place, especially the wall leading up to the spiral staircase. Photos of Nicole, the kids, his mom, his family, and friends.

We passed the spot where O.J. and Nicole used to put their Christmas tree. We passed the empty glass case that had held the Heisman. I had to go outside and sit down to regain my composure. I took a few deep breaths, and went back inside the house.

O.J. was upstairs in his bedroom, standing very still by the window. I walked in. "Are you okay?"

"Yeah."

I could not imagine what he was feeling, what that must have been like. At this point, I had genuine sympathy for him. We walked through the bedroom and went into what used to be Nicole's bathroom. Then we went downstairs, past that empty wall again. He turned back and started walking toward the living room, the formal living room. At one time he had a piano in there, with pictures of his mom, Nicole, and the kids on top of it. I remember he turned around to look at the empty room and it wasn't as though he was looking at an empty room, it was more like he was looking at a scene of what used to be there.

Then we went outside. In the concrete, near the entrance to the garage, they had carved their names "O.J. & Nicole," and their wedding date. O.J. said, "I would hate to leave this."

"Why don't you take it with you?"

This time I didn't have to persuade him. I got a circular saw, put a diamond blade on it, and cut the concrete. It took a couple of hours. O.J. would come and check my progress from time to time. To the very end, I was trying to answer his losses with a preservation of memories, as if that would make anything better or different. I am a very sentimental person in many ways, and in fact, so is O.J.

I finally managed to cut loose that piece of concrete—it was about sixteen inches long, six or seven inches wide, and four inches deep. "Here," I said, handing it to O.J.

He took it and placed it in his car. Then we did one last walk-through of the house, to see if we'd forgotten anything

Because of the commotion of the moving trucks going on around the house, the usual exit was blocked. O.J. got into his car, and I walked over and gave him an NFL football to sign. We wanted one last autograph at Rockingham. I still have that football. He backed out of the Ashford gate and drove off. After he left, a photographer went around the house, taking pictures, and the media ran their usual cruel and gleeful stories about O.J.'s misfortunes. I felt a lot of rage toward the media at this time. They claim they always take the moral high ground, but did they ever once stop to think of O.J.'s kids? This had been their home too. And for better or worse, this was their father. This was their life.

I took one last look, and then went out the gate. It closed behind me and I never looked back.

After that, O.J. and the kids moved temporarily to a house on a hill in Alta Mura, a neighborhood not far away. On a clear day, you could almost see Rockingham from there. He stayed there about a year. They kept moving. After Alta Mura, O.J. rented a house from an elderly woman whose husband was a famous actor in the 1950s. They stayed there a few months. After that house, they moved into a hotel on Sunset Boulevard, near the 405 freeway, down below the Getty museum.

Then in the winter of 1999, O.J. and the kids finally made the permanent move to Kendall, Florida, a suburb of Miami, and bought a very unremarkable, small house. He could use his pension money to purchase a house there because Florida state law protects homes from seizure by creditors. I flew down to visit him. I remember thinking, "I can't believe O.J. would live in this house." It was very nondescript, with generic furniture. There was nothing on the walls, no pictures anywhere, not even one of Nicole or the kids. It was very strange.

The house itself was probably a quarter of the size of Rockingham, with no gate, no security.

One of my last acts of trying to piece Humpty Dumpty together again, so to speak, was bringing O.J.'s stored possessions to Florida so that the house could be spruced up a little. The weekend that the Ravens won the Super Bowl, in January 2000, a friend and I arrived in Florida with a truck loaded with O.J.'s possessions from various storage units—the stuff we had pulled out of the house that panic-stricken night before the sheriff arrived.

Driving a huge moving truck, we made pickups in storage units on both coasts. All told, we crossed the United States from California to Arizona to Texas to New Orleans to Miami. We pulled up late at night in front of O.J.'s house in Kendall. O.J. came out, looked in the back of the truck, and flashed us a huge beaming smile. He was elated—now he had his home furnishings back: his dining room table, his chairs, his paintings, his lamps, and most important, his mother's piano. He was thrilled. That was the piano that his mother used to play when she would come visit him. It was the single item that meant the most to him.

We were exhausted from our cross-country adventure. We all started unpacking the stuff. I told him: "O.J., you're not going to be able to get all the paintings up."

"Why not?"

"There's more paintings than you have walls."

I could not believe how many paintings he had.

This is about the time when, although I still worked for O.J. doing signings for a few more years, we started to drift apart. I saw him less and less. I liked him less and less. He was becoming a very sordid person. When O.J. got to Florida he started regressing. He started acting like a twenty-four-year-old with no kids. He lived almost like a college student. The people he started hanging around with were people he never would have associated with before—drug-addled groupies, hangers-on, and club types. I started getting mixed up with these people too, because as his agent I had to consider some of their weird offers—everything from tabloid sting operations to O.J. partaking in a porno film.

There is one deal I wish I didn't have to tell you about, that represents the all-time low in my entire career as an agent. It's the most disgusting deal that I have ever worked on, but it would be dishonest for me to leave it out.

In January 2001, I got a phone call from a man named Don, with whom O.J. and I had done business before. Don was what I would call a seedy yet honorable guy. He called me with a very sleazy idea, concocted together with a major porno producer: They wanted O.J. to partake in a celebrity sex tape, to be shot with "hidden cameras" in a hotel room. It was to be a classic threesome, starring O.J., his girlfriend Christie Prody, and an actress/model named Patty.

They were going to pay us $2 million dollars.

Immediately blinded by the money, I, instead of dismissing it right away, started discussing the details: the money, how it would be paid under the table, what they would expect, and so forth. I don't even recall having any ethical problem with it at first, which is an indication of how low I had sunk by that time.

Once I had all the details of their proposal, I presented them to O.J.

"O.J., what do you think?" I asked.

He said, "You know, Mike, my mom being a Christian woman, with all her friends at the church, I'm just not sure I can do this to her. Those ladies at the church might *think* that I'm a killer, but if I did this movie they would *know* that I'm a porn star. I just don't think I could do that to my mom."

"O.J., listen to me," I said. "You and Christie are constantly having threesomes and having all kinds of sex all over the place and you never think about whether one day somebody is going to film you with hidden cameras. These guys I'm talking to, this is their business, this is what they do. You don't think Pamela Anderson wasn't in on her sex tape? And, if you *don't* do this, here's what is going to happen: They will, on the sly, send the hottest chick in Florida in to seduce you and Christie at some club. She and the guys who hired her will make millions, and you'll make nothing."

That gave him pause.

"Mike, I told you I couldn't do this to my mother, but let me just say this," he said. "If the money was right, and if *I didn't know about it*, and it was all set up and everything just…you know…happened…that would be a different story. Having somebody secretly film you while you're having sex doesn't make you a bad person, getting paid to star in a porno does."

This is classic O.J.—it wasn't that he didn't want to do something unethical; it was just that he wanted *deniability*.

I understood exactly what O.J. had said. I proceeded with the negotiations, kept them from O.J., and then waited for the night of the shoot to roll around.

On the night of the event, the first part of the plan went off without a hitch: O.J., Christie, and Patty all met up at the strip club. I was there too, to make sure that things went according to plan. I was anxious. My anxiety increased when I saw one of the cameramen sitting at the bar. What the hell was he doing there? I had a bolt of apprehension; I felt something just wasn't right. I went over to O.J. and told him I needed to talk to him. He didn't want to talk. "Later, Mike."

"O.J.," I said. "I need to talk to you *now*."

We went into a quiet corner.

"O.J., listen to me. Don't go into that hotel room. Don't do it. Do not go to the hotel room."

He looked kind of dazed. I wasn't sure if he heard me or not. I needed him to understand what was happening; that the thing we had discussed that he did but didn't want to know about was about to happen and that something was wrong, even by the standards of a rigged hotel porno tape situation. "Don't do anything in the room, O.J. Don't do anything." O.J. finally understood what I was saying and he knew what was going on. He went up to the room, but told me he was just going to hang out.

I felt sweat trickling into my ears. I thought I was going to vomit. I didn't know until later that O.J. had already handled it. He'd walked more or less right over to the small bushy plant that held the main camera— the size of a thumbnail—and turned it around to face the wall.

I called O.J.'s cell. He answered. "Damn, Mike, what the fuck's going on?

"O.J., did you do anything in the room?"

"No," he said. "Don't worry."

"O.J., this was the deal we talked about. You understood that, right? Listen to me…did they get *anything*?"

"No, man. They didn't."

He was very relaxed about it all. I, as usual, was having a heart attack.

"Mike," he said, laughing, "give me a couple of weeks to work out, and get rid of my beer gut, then let's do this right, let's shoot it down in the Bahamas. But let's do this shit *right*."

We never did.

His girlfriend, Christie Prody—a young woman with insatiable appetites for drugs, sex, threesomes, and trouble—was always in the middle of the various schemes. Christie was and is his partner in debauchery. She was twenty-one when he met her. She was what we called a "curb girl." She cruised the street in Rockingham until she caught O.J.'s eye. Christie is like everybody else around O.J. now. She has poor judgment.

They live for the day, for the next sensation. O.J. would not have hung out with these people before.

I thought he was going to start his life over, and try to come back to society somehow, but he went the other way. He surrounded himself with unsavory people. I had never, until after the verdict, been to a strip club with O.J., never seen him smoke pot or do coke, never seen him talk about threesomes, ecstasy—all these things that he and Christie got into. He was doing things worse than Nicole ever thought of doing. He would say that he was "sue proof," and that anybody who wanted to sue him could get in line behind the Goldmans.

Naturally, I feel most sorry for the kids. I wish they had stayed with the Browns, even though I am no fan of the Browns. I worry about the kids deeply—mostly Sydney. Justin actually seemed pretty well-adjusted, strangely enough. He was pretty young when all this happened. Sydney wasn't so young. Whenever I went to the house in Florida and O.J. would enter the room, she would roll her eyes and leave for her room. For the most part that's where she would stay.

Sydney and I had been close. I felt like she needed more attention and understanding, and I think she recognized that I cared about her. I knew her life must have been miserable. Her mother was dead and her father put himself, not the kids, first. Sydney absolutely hated Christie Prody—and with good reason.

It wasn't like the old days, at all, with housekeepers preparing meals, hustle and bustle, and life. There was always tension in Florida. O.J. told me that he couldn't wait for Sydney to get out of the house and go to college. He always said, "She's just like her fucking mother. So much drama with her." He was more interested in being Christie Prody's boyfriend than in being Sydney's father.

I said to him once, "O.J., imagine what it's like to be Sydney. Imagine what it's like, first, to be *any* teenager in high school these days. You get teased for whatever your parents are or do, whatever they can find to pick on you about. Not only is Sydney a teenage girl, but her dad is on the cover of a tabloid every couple of months. Imagine the pressure she is under. Do you think that all of her friends' parents say, 'Oh, sure, you can go sleep over at Sydney's house?'

"Why would they want Sydney to be around their kids? Eighty-five percent of the country thinks you're a killer. Imagine what it's like, O.J., to see that stuff, and to see that *you don't care*. You just get right back into bed with Christie Prody, no matter how bad you make yourself look in the tabloids, like a photo of Christie with a knife saying you told her, 'I killed Nicole.'"

I think that tabloid story was an inside deal between Christie and O.J. They always had her go sell stories to the tabloids, then they'd split the money.

"Sydney sees this. She is sitting there thinking, 'Why can't you put me first? Why can't you just be a dad like everybody else's dad?' O.J., *my* kids were embarrassed by it when *I* was in the tabloids because of you."

He would just sit there and listen. I would always proffer my opinion to him. I wasn't a yes man. But he really didn't say anything much. He was just oblivious. It didn't matter. When I would bring up the Christie factor, asking, "Why does Sydney's opinion have so little value to you?" he would just brush it off, saying, "Sydney's fine, Mike." But she was not fine. She was starting to get into trouble. I found that, among other things, she'd taken up smoking (she was still in high school).

She came home one day, and I met her on the patio. I gave her a kiss on the head. "Hi, sweetheart, how are you?" I got around to asking her how long she'd been smoking.

"For a while."

"Is everything okay?"

She looked in to where O.J. was. "*No*."

I never saw much tenderness from O.J. toward her. And though she was a very good athlete, O.J. never seemed very interested. He didn't make much of a point of turning up for her basketball or volleyball games— although he did attend more often in Florida than he had in California. O.J. once asked me to go pick her up from a game, and it was then, seeing all the other parents and their children, that it really hit me; I really missed Nicole. She would have been there, in the stands, clapping for Sydney, beaming with pride. I felt so sorry for Sydney, seeing all the other mothers and fathers watching their kids. Nicole, if she were alive, would have been there to watch every game, whereas O.J. would have slept in. Nicole once remarked to Faye that she felt so sad for Justin that he had a world-famous athlete for a dad but he never once tossed a ball in the yard with him.

O.J.'s relationship with Sydney was more than sad. The two of them would get in foul-mouthed shouting matches that were embarrassing to watch.

O.J. once said to me, "Justin and I can get along. We don't have all that emotion. Sydney always has to have an attitude. She's *disrespectful*, just like her mother."

I wanted to say, "O.J., what is Sydney disrespectful *of*? Think about that for a while."

I didn't like the way O.J. treated Sydney, but when people ask me why I finally broke ties with O.J., the best answer I can give is that O.J. betrayed *me*. Year in, year out, I was there for him, covered for him, got him out of jams, even lied for him. And when O.J. was deposed in the civil trial, what did he do? He threw me under the bus about fifty times in one deposition. Every time he was asked about any of his financial or professional dealings, he said, "I have no idea. Ask Mike Gilbert." He would make it all seem like I was at fault and he was pure as the driven snow.

He wanted me to shelter money for him, and nagged me until I finally broke down and did it. This happened both in L.A. and in Florida, and each time I was left holding the bag. Every time O.J. had an appearance he had to be paid under the table in cash, because otherwise the Goldmans would get it. Do you realize how many people have assisted in the effort to keep O.J.'s money safe from the Goldmans? Trust me, it takes a village. I would always take O.J.'s payment as my own, and then send it to him.

"Eventually somebody has to take the hit on this," I'd say.

He always said, "We'll take care of it later." But later never came. In the meantime, I got hammered with taxes. Somebody had to pay them. For every gig O.J. took, I got 20 percent—which I paid taxes on, and then I still owe taxes on O.J.'s 80 percent. I was losing money on every job we did. When I pushed it, he said, "Hey, at least you don't owe $33.5 million dollars."

"Yeah, I didn't kill anybody either."

O.J. gave me a scowl, a fuck-you look. But I was pissed off and tired of being his fall guy. In 2006, I had finally had enough. It happened just like that. One day I just decided to cross over the border and defect, to see if I could find freedom on the other side.

I called O.J. and told him I didn't want to represent him anymore, that I was done. Then I hung up.

I called Greta Van Susteren and told her what had been going on, and she invited me on her show to talk about it. In that interview, I said flat out that O.J. was guilty, and described what kind of person my former hero actually was. I said, "O.J. is the kind of guy who would take life preservers from his own children if they were all on the *Titanic*. He cares about himself and only himself. He is incapable of love."

I called O.J. before the show and told him to watch it and he said he would. Afterward he called me right away. "Why would you say those things," he said.

"O.J., for the first time, I am saying what I believe, what I am feeling—not what you believe." He kept calling but I never picked up his calls after that.

I haven't spoken to him since.

CHAPTER FIFTEEN

FEAR AND LOATHING IN LAS VEGAS

On the night of September 13, 2007, O.J., accompanied by four accomplices, burst into a room in the Palace Station hotel in Las Vegas in a blind fury, in pursuit of various items he felt had been stolen from him. He can be heard on audio tapes subsequently posted at a gossip channel's Web site, screaming: *Think you can take my shit and sell it, motherfuckers? . . . Don't let nobody out of this room, motherfucker. You think you can take my shit and sell it?*

"No," says a meek male voice. O.J. continues to bellow and scream.

Then the meek voice cuts into the din again and says, "Mike took it."

O.J. roars, "*I know fucking Mike took it.*"

The Mike in question is me. The guy who says, "Mike took it," is my old buddy Bruce Fromong, a fellow memorabilia collector who had been my friend for twenty years, until, that is, he absconded with the entire contents of my storage unit and tried to sell it all that day in Vegas. He planned to run away with one of his girlfriends, but instead landed in the hospital with a heart attack.

We have now arrived at the grand finale, and things are beginning to become more comic.

If character is destiny, and I think it is, the Las Vegas episode is where we learn our fate.

I have come to a point in life where I figure I may as well just tell the truth and see what happens.

The background of the Las Vegas episode is so preposterous, I trust you will believe me when I say I could not make this up.

It all began with the suit.

I mentioned before that O.J. gave me his "lucky suit"—the one he was wearing when he was acquitted, the morning after he got out of jail, in October of 1995. That suit is in one of my storage units. It has been taken out on a few road trips when I came close to selling it. I have the suit, the shirt he was wearing, and the tie—the whole ensemble. O.J. asked me about it a few years ago, wondering if I still had it. He said he had been offered good money for it by Madame Tussaud's. "Too fucking bad," I said with a smile. "Yes, I still have it."

I also collected, over the years, many other valuable items that fell into my path in the storm that wrecked O.J.'s life, but none of it was taken without his knowledge and consent. I had everything from cards to photos to books to footballs to jerseys—you name it.

I never once took anything without checking with O.J. I have been questioned in Las Vegas and no charges of any kind were made that I had taken anything from O.J. without his consent.

The Vegas story is much more pathetic than tragic. I'll tell it to you from the very beginning, from where I got on this bus to where I got off. I know the central characters in this debacle very well. I could easily have been in that hotel room myself, because there were so many hundreds of times Bruce and I were in hotel rooms across the country selling O.J.

memorabilia. But that was behind me now. I had broken with O.J., and I had gotten tired of the memorabilia business.

The first person you need to know about is Al Beardsley. The first time I was introduced to Al Beardsley was during the criminal trial. He contacted me through Skip Taft with a message that he wanted to buy some O.J. memorabilia. He bought a few low-end items—some photographs, jerseys, and footballs.

Beardsley was also a trial groupie. He was one of the guys who hung out around the courtroom during the criminal trial in hopes of being drawn for the lottery where people could win a seat at the trial. When I first met him, he said he was an assistant manager at a movie theater that showed old classic films. I believe he made his living by taking movies that were going to be destroyed from old theaters and selling them.

The more I got to know Al Beardsley, the more I found him to be unstable, to put it mildly. He was placed in a mental facility at one point because (among other things) he grew convinced that everybody who had their headlights on during the day in Burbank was sending him a message that they wanted him to run for mayor. He was going through a psychosis at the time, and used to call me from the hospital and leave wildly delusional messages. They were so bizarre, I started saving them.

In one of them he explained that he saw a car on the freeway and realized it was O.J. and started chasing him. When he finally caught up with him, he said O.J. turned into a white guy right in front of his eyes.

Messages like that made me realize I needed to distance myself from Beardsley. I told my associate Bruce Fromong that I wanted nothing to do with Beardsley and that if he were involved with any potential deal, Bruce should not even call me about it. It would have been a waste of my time, if for no other reason than that Beardsley was in and out of living facilities for the homeless. I didn't like nor trust Al Beardsley.

Meanwhile, I turned down offers from people who wanted to buy the "lucky suit" in order to burn it. I always thought it was pretty amazing what some people would pay to destroy an object and imagine that they were destroying O.J.

Bruce and I tried to sell the suit on eBay at one point, but that kept falling through because of the blood fleck on the collar. (You can't sell anything with biological matter on eBay.)

In January 2007, I got a call from Bruce, saying he had two guys from Burbank who were very interested in buying the suit for between $25,000 and $50,000, and that they wanted to meet us in Vegas. I said I might accept $40,000, cash.

I drove myself and the suit to Las Vegas to meet Bruce, and, supposedly, the prospective buyers. We went to have the suit notarized in my name, and I remember Bruce started acting a little fishy. First, he was insisting that we should get it notarized in his name as well, because our buyers didn't like me, supposedly—whoever they were.

Bruce and I sat around various restaurants and bars, killing time, waiting for these clowns to turn up. Bruce kept pretending his cell phone wasn't ringing properly for some reason, yet he was supposedly getting messages from them explaining why they were late. Supposedly they were having dinner. They never did turn up, and that was the end of that. I started putting together the odd events of the day and I began to question Bruce's trustworthiness. It was a wasted trip, and I headed home, and said to myself, the hell with all this bullshit. I can sell the suit myself without the help of Bruce.

I now have to tell you about something that sounds very dull, namely the history of my storage space in Hanford, California, which is the trigger for the whole event.

I kept a storage space for years that had a lot of O.J. items in it, including about 3,000 signed copies of O.J.'s book *I Want to Tell You*. Before the Goldman judgment came down, O.J. asked me to move the books from a public storage unit in Los Angeles to a safer place. I loaded them into a truck, took them to Hanford, and put them into storage there. I had lots of O.J. memorabilia in this unit, as well as memorabilia from Bo Jackson, Marcus Allen, Tim Brown, and many others.

One day I got a call from Beardsley, who said that he had gotten my storage unit number by calling the storage facility and claiming to be me trying to pay the bill. God only knows how many storage facilities he had to call before he stumbled onto the right one. I told you, Beardsley is nuts. Anyway, I called my friend Christy Lutkemeier, and asked if she would put a storage unit under her name, which she did. I went straight over to my unit and packed everything up and moved it to the unit in her name. One day I went to get something in the storage unit, and everything was gone. I called Christy. She said she had been trying to reach me to tell me that the account was so delinquent they had a second lien on the storage unit. This had placed so much pressure on her that she had called Bruce Fromong—thinking that we were still friends and unaware of my new doubts about his trustworthiness—and asked him to help her move the stuff out and keep it for me.

Christy and Bruce met up the next day at the storage facility, cut the lock off my storage unit, and removed all the stuff. Bruce drove off with it all packed in his black Ford pickup, and reassured Christy that he would keep it safe for me. When I finally spoke to her, Christy told me it was safe.

Bruce, meanwhile, had his own personal problems. Bruce had two girlfriends at the time . . . and a wife. He planned to dump his wife for one of them, Loretta, but would have dumped his wife and her for the other one, Lacy, if she'd give him the time of day. Loretta had been Bruce's girl-friend for many years, and had dumped him and started seeing another guy. So Bruce, trying to lure Loretta back, hatched a plot. He told her he could raise $100,000 by selling off all this O.J. memorabilia in Vegas, and that they would then take the money and live in Boston.

Lacy, meanwhile, the woman of Bruce's dreams, is the recipient of his frequent boozy boasts about the riches he possesses in the form of O.J. memorabilia. One day I got a call from Lacy, asking me if I knew that Bruce had all my stuff and was getting ready to sell it all and move with Loretta to Boston. At first I wanted to laugh, because this was so utterly Bruce-like and crazy. Then again, what did I expect? It all made perfect sense in its absurd way.

I called Bruce, got his voicemail, and left a message: "Bruce, you need to call me back because if you have my shit I want it back *and if you sold it, I want the money.*"

Then I called Christy and told her what Bruce had done. She became very upset. She called Bruce, and said, "What's this about you selling Mike's stuff?"

He said, "I can't talk now. . . . I'm in a meeting."

Bruce, at that time, was in a hotel room in Vegas loaded with O.J. memorabilia, much of it mine, anticipating that a high-end memorabilia dealer was going to come in and buy it all, because Beardsley, of all people, had told him so.

Christy suddenly heard, over the phone, wild commotion, screaming and cussing, as O.J. and his gun-toting thugs came bursting into the room. Auctioneer Thomas Riccio had rigged the entire thing, double-crossing everybody and laying a trap for O.J. Riccio had told O.J. that there were "thousands" of memorabilia items in that room, as well as his "lucky suit," which was not true. Riccio taped the whole thing, then sold the tape to tabloid TV and arranged an immunity deal for himself. Bruce, in a telling detail, called the tabloid TV shows after all this went down, but *before* he called 911.

Beardsley tried to scramble out of the mess by stating he was on O.J.'s side and wanted all charges of robbery dropped. Bruce Fromong proceeded to have a heart attack from the stress and was hospitalized. His long-suffering wife sat by his side, not knowing that he had planned to leave her and run away with Loretta. I called Bruce when I heard this and left him a message: "Bruce, don't go die of a heart attack now. We'll figure out what the right thing is to do here and we'll get it done." He never called me back and I haven't spoken to him since.

Christy, who heard parts of the incident on the phone (until O.J.'s accomplices hung up Bruce's phone and left the room with boxes of memorabilia), will be a crucial witness in the Las Vegas trial—she is what's known as an "ear witness."

O.J., as you may know, is up on charges of armed robbery, kidnapping, and ten other felony charges, with the trial date set for September 2008. The stuff that was taken out of the room (that belongs to me) is now in the possession of the police.

O.J. told the police he believed there were pictures of his mother and various family mementos in that room. This whole mess is rooted in the chaos that ensued on the night we packed up Rockingham, before the sheriff's office and Fred Goldman's movers were due to come over in the morning. Everything left Rockingham, but where did it go and who kept track of it? Things went all over the place, into storage under various names. Some were stored under "Orenthal Productions," some went under O.J.'s mother's name, some under the name of one of his sisters, some went to my storage, and several high-dollar items and various trophies and awards went to an attorney and friend of O.J.'s sister. When O.J.'s mother died in 2001, the bills for the storage unit that were in her name were left unpaid, and eventually the contents were put up for public auction. Beardsley lied and told Riccio to tell O.J. that he had magically found all of O.J.'s lost goods, that he had "thousands and thousands" of items. The truth is that a lot of it is simply gone, lost.

I was flown to Vegas to offer my testimony about the origins of the items in mid-December 2007. There are no charges against me. O.J. always knew what I had in my locker, it was never a secret. Beardsley has subsequently filed a lawsuit against Riccio. And Fromong has apparently had a second heart attack, in February 2008.

I am told that when O.J. came into that room in Las Vegas, he was expecting me to be there. That would have been an interesting reunion. I was asked by a reporter if I was surprised by the rage heard on the audio tape from the hotel room in Las Vegas. I said not at all. That is the same rage Nicole heard the night of October 25, 1993—as well as the many other times she called the police over their seventeen-year relationship. If you listen to the 911 call you can hear the same voice with the same rage—it's O.J. Simpson. I often wonder how many times people will dial 911 because of O.J. and his temper. Since the night of the murders, O.J.'s current girlfriend Christie Prody has dialed 911 on at least two occasions and even his and Nicole's daughter, Sydney, has dialed 911 because of him.

The irony is not lost on me, nor is the tragedy: the suit that O.J. was acquitted in, the suit he always considered "lucky," might become the same suit that would possibly land him in jail for the rest of his life. Then again, we don't know that O.J. will go to jail. To be honest with you, I'd be surprised if he did.

CHAPTER SIXTEEN

REFLECTIONS

If I had known what a torrent of emotions would come up as a result of writing this book, I probably would never have undertaken it. I have revisited every mistake—without the ability to change a single one.

I don't just relay these things as distant memories—every time I recount what happened, I go back there, back through the corridor of time, and I actually relive the emotions, sensations, sights, sounds, and smells. My memory is merciless: I can remember moments with O.J. down to the last detail. I remember what song was playing on the radio, what each person ordered to eat, and what everybody was wearing. I relive my own actions and, in almost each case, I regret my decisions. They were all born from the original mistake, and after that, each choice was a futile attempt to shore up or compensate for the one before and the one before that.

I am sitting here in my publisher's office, looking out over Washington, D.C., alone. The book is finished, and I'm realizing that I didn't get the one thing I wanted, which was peace of mind. Instead I am swimming in regrets, and they're not too few to mention:

I regret the vilification of the Goldman family, which I partook in. I regret not going to Nicole's grave, if only by myself, just to tell her that I know the truth and that I am sorry. I regret being blinded by celebrity and money, by O.J.'s immense charisma, and my hero-worship of him. I regret prioritizing and caring about *what* I was, an agent, instead of *who* I was, Mike Gilbert, and not having the character to do the right thing. I regret trying to do the most foolish thing in the world, which is to argue with reality. You know what? Reality always wins.

O.J., it seems, can go on forever, play golf, smile and just bury it all. I can't.

It must be very difficult for O.J., to have been a hero, to have been idolized, and now to be loathed. I remember sitting with him once, and talking about what will happen when each of us dies. When I die, I will be a footnote to O.J.'s life story. When he dies, people will celebrate. They will actually be happy. They will deface his tombstone. Imagine what it's like to be hated like that.

I'm thinking about the saying: "Be careful what you wish for, because you might get it."

Remember, when I was in the eighth grade I wanted to *be* O.J. Simpson, never mind wanting to meet him. I feel that in a very mysterious way, the gods heard me. I have in many ways become O.J., but not the part of him that I admired. I have been one step behind him for almost twenty years, trying to carry, save, redeem, and analyze his soul. Over time, I lost all my boundaries. It was the football hero I started out trying to protect and preserve, but in the end it was the real O.J., the man behind the mask, whom I wound up merging with, battling with, and finally succumbing to.

People always ask the same thing when they find out my history. As soon as they hear about my relationship to him, they ask two questions. First they ask, "Did he do it?" Then they ask, "Why would you represent someone you know murdered two people?"

I generally ignored the first question, but always answered the second one. My answer has perhaps become threadbare over the years, but I still believe it and still stand by it. I quote a movie about murder, crime, and punishment. The line I quote is spoken by Susan Sarandon's character in *Dead Man Walking*. She is a nun who stands for mercy and says, "I will not judge a man by the worst day of his life."

I still don't judge O.J. solely by what he did on June 12, 1994. That was the worst day of his life. I believe in mercy, forgiveness, and redemption. For my part, after the murders, after the trial, I was prepared to give O.J. another chance.

But in the thousands of days that have followed since, O.J. has thrown away that second chance, and revealed himself to be something I didn't want to see. I started to see it during the criminal trial—what type of father he really was, what type of friend he really was, the way he increasingly only cared about his own welfare and the impression he could make on people.

I am judging him now on the sum total of his daily life—the way he treated Nicole, the way he treats his kids, his friends, and his girlfriend, who was recently hospitalized, bleeding from the brain and with head-to-toe bruises. *Of course* O.J. had nothing to do with it. Haven't you heard? She "fell" at a gas station. As somebody remarked, she must have fallen *on* the gas station while being hurled from a car driving seventy miles an hour to have such bruises.

This whole incident has somehow been swept under the carpet, which is probably how Christie Prody herself wants it, which was also how Nicole wanted it, and how Nicole's whole family wanted it. Anything at all to avoid making O.J. look at himself.

Look at the guys in Las Vegas O.J. had just met—they could wind up going to prison because of him. Everyone is a pawn who is sacrificed for O.J.

Everyone.

My biggest regret is that I put my loyalty and my commitment to him before that which mattered most: my family. I owe them—my wife and my kids—my biggest apology.

How I did my job destroyed us.

People always used to say to me: You have the best job, you get to fly everywhere first-class, go to any game you want, you live like a rock star.

But it's a mirage; it's Disneyland. While you're there, the world's problems go away. You're walking around in Disneyland and Mickey Mouse, or Goofy, is waving to you. But inside those costumes are working people, fighting for a raise, trying to feed their family—who knows.

There are those of us who haven't lived the life that we wish we had or made the decisions we wish we had made. The worst part about the attacks that are coming now, toward me, is that a lot of what they say is true. That is all I can say in response.

I didn't have one clear breaking point with O.J. Sure, there was that one day I finally made up my mind, but preceding that was a gradual erosion of faith and respect for both O.J. and myself that took place over many years. I was tired of seeing how he never learned anything, never tried to change, never tried to understand how any of his actions had caused the nightmare we were living. O.J. always came first. O.J. always had to come across as innocent, flawless, misunderstood, while everybody else—especially Nicole—was to blame. When I witnessed how he put himself and his debauchery with Christie Prody before the welfare of his kids, I truly became disgusted.

When I first started managing O.J. there was a clear line of right and wrong. During the criminal trial, things started to fall into a gray area that got wider and wider. Eventually everything wound up in the gray area. Things he did, things I did, it was all just *wrong*. The further O.J. got from the counsel and guidance of Skip Taft, the worse everything got. Few of his decisions were good anymore. He was orchestrating his own final downfall.

Nothing was out of bounds, nothing was ethically or morally wrong if the price was right. It became depressing, and finally, asphyxiating.

I hope I can move on. I want to pick up the pieces of my life and put them back together again.

I want to live a simple life and start over. There is no place I could go where nobody has heard of O.J. Simpson, but I'd like to go where they don't associate the two of us, where I can put my past behind me.

The turning point for me was that dream I had about my grandmother, one of the most vivid dreams I have ever had. In the dream, she told me to return to who I was when I was a little boy.

Thinking about my grandmother made me remember something that is simply, for once, a good memory of O.J.

My grandmother was very old, and living in a skilled nursing facility in Hanford. O.J. came to Hanford with me one day shortly before she died, in 2003, to visit her. She was excited. She said, "Mike, be sure to take O.J. to Superior Dairy and buy him a milkshake." Superior Dairy is a wonderful old ice cream parlor in the central square of Hanford that has been there since the 1930s, with pink stools and pastel walls. The central square of Hanford looks like the town square in the *Back to the Future* movies. It has a town clock, an old-fashioned movie marquee, and there on the corner, the Superior Dairy ice cream parlor. I walked around with O.J. and showed him all the sights. He wanted to go into the little antique shop. We were in there for a good while, looking around. O.J. found a little lamp, a small replica of a Tiffany lamp. He said, "I think your grandmother would like that." He bought it for her and they wrapped it up. She loved it. O.J. plugged it in and it sat on her hospital bedside table until her death. She was so touched that O.J. came to see her. She was absolutely queen for a day. That was the side of O.J. that I remembered before the murders. He *was* kind, he *was* considerate. Like all of us, he was a lot of things.

I was asked recently if I wished I had never met O.J. and I was surprised to hear myself answer, "No."

We had a lot of good times, and I learned a lot. I don't wish I'd never met him. Why? Because he showed me reality. This was my life.

I learned a very valuable lesson and it took me a long time to learn it.

The slow and painful lesson that I finally learned is who my real heroes are. My heroes are my father, grandmother, and grandfather. Not some superstar, some idol.

The past fourteen years have been an almost unrelenting hell, but if I really had to choose, I wouldn't choose another life. I remember one night after O.J. got out of jail, we went for a drive and I played a song by Garth Brooks called "The Dance." Gretchen was with us. The theme of the song is: if we knew how things would turn out, would we change it? You may miss out on some of the pain, but you'd also have to miss the joy, the dance.

I asked him, "O.J., if you could change it, if you could change it all, and never have met Nicole, never have fallen in love with her, never have had that first kiss with her, never have had kids with her, never have had any of it, would you change it?"

We listened to its lyrics about love, pain, and loss. After the song was over we sat quietly. Gretchen understood what I was asking him—*she* got it.

O.J. said, "Mike, if I didn't feel like killing myself before, I do now."

I can't answer this question for O.J., but I can answer it for myself.

I wouldn't change it.

I still believe that we are all here for a reason and the reason is to learn how to be human. Some of us fall and stumble worse than others. Some of us make terrible mistakes and some of us make less terrible mistakes. I made truly terrible mistakes, but those mistakes were my life and were my reality—my lessons. They were all learned within a framework of some kind of love, or aspiration. The classic theme here is that we worshipped false idols, false gods. We reached for the glittering things that would be our downfall, rather than the true things we could build lives from. It was a hell of a ride, and it was a ride to hell.

We may admire people who don't make mistakes, but we learn a lot more from those who do. O.J. did everything that was in his character to do. So did I. I keep finding that every time I harbor extreme judgment about somebody, it's because I recognize something of myself in their behavior. I have spent years attacking and vilifying other people—mainly the Goldmans and the Browns—because we were at war, we were under siege, we were trying to defend our own camp, and we never had time to stop and think, reflect, choose the right response, reach for the higher instinct.

My first spoken words when I heard that Nicole had been murdered were: "He finally did it." When Denise Brown first heard that her sister had been murdered, she yelled something like: "It's O.J.! *Find O.J. He did it.*"

It occurs to me now that this means that *we* did it too. If we were so certain that O.J. had killed Nicole, then that means we knew he might, we knew he could, we knew he was just one bad day away from actually doing it. And what did any of us do about it? Absolutely nothing. That includes me, and many people who, unlike me, were actually close to Nicole, and knew what she was going through—her family, her best friends, A.C., Marcus—everybody. A.C. took Nicole to the hospital after one of her beatings. Denise saw her sister bruised and battered many times (she probably even saw the very first black eye O.J. gave Nicole, when she was just a teenager—the one he gave her the Ferrari to atone for). How many beatings, eruptions, bruises, and 911 calls did we need before we did something? Nobody stepped in and tried to take her out of the situation. We just pretended it hadn't happened or wasn't significant. O.J. mattered more. His image mattered more. The fringe benefits that came with being one of O.J.'s friends mattered more—or at least we thought they did.

I never listened to Nicole's side of the story. I never asked her. I didn't care. O.J. was my client. That right there—that's human nature for you. Many of us see what we want to see and act out of self-interest. We tell ourselves that we have to look out for number one and we make sure not to rock the boat just so long as we're the ones who are sitting comfortably in it. How often do any of us stick our necks out for another human being who is in trouble and needs our help? Not often enough, I fear.

I listen now to Nicole's 911 call, from October 25, 1993, and I hear it completely differently from when I heard it during the trial. I always heard it through O.J.'s constant self-serving spin—that Nicole was drunk, and angry, and out of control. Listening to it today, the person I hear on that tape is neither drunk, nor angry, nor out of control. She is *afraid*. She is terrified for her life and for her children. Nicole at one point says, "He's O.J. Simpson. I think you know his record."

Well, I didn't know his record, and I was his agent and friend. I didn't want to know. That's the sad thing. Sometimes we hide from knowledge that we fear will be burdensome. I once negotiated for O.J. to appear at a function in Bakersfield for battered women. They called me and said, "He had an altercation, in 1989, what do you know about that?"

I called O.J. and of course he just gave me the spin—Nicole was drunk, she started it, the usual. I took him at his word. I never took the time to care. I wanted to believe him and so I did—and so did the people organizing the function for battered women. That was the function, remember, that Nicole didn't allow O.J. to book. I never really knew why she didn't let him go, and her "we're going to the zoo" explanation never sat quite right with me. When I look back now, knowing what I do, I think that Nicole simply couldn't bear the hypocrisy of having her abusive husband headlining a function for battered women.

A lot of people in his inner circle *did* know his record, especially those close to Nicole. I wonder: How do those people feel? How much guilt do they have? How about Nicole's family? How about Marcus? How about A.C.?

And how about me?

Did I really help O.J. get away with murder?

Yes. But it wasn't just by suggesting he not take his arthritis medicine. I never did what I now wish I had, what nobody ever did: defended Nicole. A lot of people could have intervened early on, but like ostriches with our heads stuck in the sand, we ignored the obvious. Only one man, I believe, did have the courage to stand up to O.J.: Ronald Goldman. He gave his life defending Nicole, while the rest of us just sat idly by, counting our money.

None of us were there the night of June 12, but I truly believe any one of us could have prevented the murders. When, after all, did the killing start? Did it start the first time he hit Nicole, or locked her in a closet, or called her a fat bitch? When? I don't know, but I'm damn sure it was sometime before June 12, 1994.

He did it. But he couldn't have done it without us.

I'm not the only one who helped O.J. get away with murder. But I hope to be the first to finally confess.

I know it's too late. But at the same time, I hope it's not.

In closing I'd like to make some apologies. I am sorry, Mr. Goldman, for the loss of your son and for how I treated you in your time of mourning. Kim Goldman, I'm sorry that you couldn't have your brother at your wedding, and that you can't call him or hug him or tell him that you love him. Sharon Rufo, I know you didn't really have a relationship with your son and I'm sorry that you will never have the opportunity to develop one. And, to Nicole's parents and siblings, I disagree with some of the things you have done since the murders, but I am nevertheless sorry for your loss. Sydney and Justin, I'm sorry that your mother was taken away from you, and that you had to grow up in the middle of all of this pain. I apologize to all of you, not just for allowing the murders to take place, or for treating you poorly after the murders, but for failing to come clean sooner, and for refusing to help bring O.J. to justice.

I hope to apologize to Nicole and Ron some day too . . . face to face. My only hope is that I can do enough between now and then to warrant their forgiveness.

ACKNOWLEDGMENTS

So many people have contributed so much to my life, and I'd like to thank all of them. Time and space restrictions being what they are, though, I cannot name them all. They know who they are, and I trust they know they have my thanks.

As far as those I can name, I'd like to begin by thanking my family. My children Michael, David, Chrissy, Luke, and Lindsay all grew up during the chaos that was the aftermath of the murders, and though that was very difficult for them at times, they have all become wonderful human beings. I love them very much. I'd like to thank my two daughters-in-law too, Margaret and Mary (welcome to the family). My siblings have also stuck with me through all of this mess (thank you Debbie, Sondra, and Larry). My grandparents, Jack and Iris, though not with us anymore, were crucially involved in my upbringing (I am deeply saddened that I, for a time, drifted so far from their teachings). My father, Richard, has been with me my entire life and has always been a pillar of strength. I hope that I can offer him even half the encouragement and support that he has offered me in my times of need now that he finds himself in a difficult time of his own (Dad, we'll beat this cancer together). To my stepmother, Dorothy, I don't know why I call you "stepmother." I love you and am proud that you are my mother.

When it comes to my family, I owe the most thanks to my beautiful wife, Debbie. She, as is mentioned in this book, went through an especially dark and difficult time as a result of being so close to the madness. She is strong though, and she has found her way back into the light. I would also like to thank Debbie's family for being so supportive, my late father-in-law Howard, my mother-in-law Phyllis, and Kathy, Kyle, Kristy, Kelly, Kent, Lynn, Keith, Amy, and Kelly.

I'd like to thank Skip Taft; though he and I no longer speak (and have not for far too long), I'd like to thank him simply because he's such a good human being. When I get down and think that everyone is self-serving and that nobody is altruistic or kind, I think of Skip and my hope in humanity is restored.

Special thanks to Tracy Mattos for her encouragement and support. Her help and research on this project were absolutely invaluable.

Greta Van Susteren has guided me and counseled me these past several years, and I owe her a huge debt of gratitude.

Many thanks are owed to Christy Lutkemeier, a close friend who has helped me in countless ways over the past several years.

Thanks to Angie Stanland, Julie Green, and Tammy Neros of the Kansas City Hyatt Regency for all of their support during the trial.

I know a few professional athletes who understand that they have been given a gift. They are humble and thankful for the opportunity to play the game, and don't consider themselves above the law and better than everybody else. They are good people and they should be role models for all of us. It is athletes like them who allow me to continue watching and enjoying professional sports and I thank them for that. I have often been asked who my favorite pro-athlete is. That's easy to answer. . . . Tim Brown. If all of my children can grow up to be as kind, compassionate, and giving as Tim Brown, then I would be very proud.

I owe a special debt of gratitude to all of the wonderful people at Regnery Publishing. Thank you Jeff Carneal, president of Eagle Publishing, Marji Ross, president and publisher of Regnery Publishing, and Harry Crocker, executive editor. I had the special pleasure of working closely with Marji and am grateful to her for her care and advice. Thank you John Lalor for championing this book. I'd like to thank my editor, Miriam Moore. I could not have written this book without her talent, dedication to the project, and tireless effort. This was an important but difficult book for me to write, and Miriam not only made the process easier, but was also a calming influence during the long hours and stressful times. Her associates Kate Frantz and Christian Tappe helped ably in this effort. I'd like to thank Kathleen Mitchell and Jeanne Crotty for their hard work in promoting this book, and Amanda Larsen, Amber Colleran, and Kristina Phillips for their fine work in preparing the text and the photographs. And last, thanks to Karen Woodard for her assistance.

My great admiration and gratitude also go to my son David. His efforts on this book were inestimable. He gave up his own time to come to Washington to help me on the final leg of this project. I am forever grateful to him for the time he devoted to the project, his indispensable contributions, and for the opportunity to share this experience with him. David, you made me very proud.

And finally, I'd like to thank Celia Farber for her untiring and unyielding help on this project. I met her when she was assigned as a reporter to cover O.J., and she has become a friend. This book would (literally) never have been written if it weren't for her. Thank you so much, Celia.

APPENDIX I

HOW IT ALL WENT DOWN

I think I know how it happened. Throughout the criminal and civil trials, it was as though a film was being created in my mind one frame at a time. I base this statement "I think I know how it happened," on knowing him, knowing her, having been to each of their houses, listening to every single bit of testimony, and having had fourteen years to think about it.

On June 12, O.J. went to Sydney's dance recital. Nicole shunned him. She didn't save him a seat at the recital and didn't invite him to dinner with the family at Mezzaluna. He used to say to me, "Why would I be bothered about not being invited to Mezzaluna? It wasn't even a good restaurant. I don't need to go there."

That's typical of O.J.'s one-man spin machine. It's absurd, like so many things he says. The food at Mezzaluna wasn't the point, being exiled from the family was—and Nicole made that exile plain.

In the past, no matter how much they fought, O.J. had always been able to buy Nicole back. He couldn't *tell* her he was sorry but he could *show* her. But about three weeks before the murders, Nicole returned two gifts O.J. had given her—a pair of very expensive diamond earrings and a bracelet. Once she returned those gifts, he knew it was over for real. No matter what he says, in those final weeks, he was the one chasing her. And by the night of the murders, he was seething with rage from her rejection.

Earlier that day, O.J. had a blowout argument with Paula Barbieri, his girl-friend at the time, because he wouldn't let her come to the dance recital. So she flew to Las Vegas to meet with Michael Bolton. O.J. called her, repeatedly, even at her hotel. She never answered her phone. He started calling all the women he knew, but none of them were available or were willing to change their plans to see him.

O.J.'s greatest fear was of rejection. And on June 12, 1994, he was getting a full dose of it. He raged to Kato Kaelin, his houseguest, about how "inappropriate" Nicole's clothing was, too sexy, too young. He realized that she was still hot, still beautiful, but she was not *his*. What is the line in the Dwight Yoakam song where he says a woman never looks so good as when she's walking out the door?

I think Nicole was really happy to be Nicole Brown again, maybe for the first time in years. If you read her last letter to O.J., she had not loved him for a long time. She had had enough. She was ready to move on with her life. But O.J. wasn't ready to let her go.

| | | | | | |

When Ron Goldman got off work at Mezzaluna at 9:33 PM, he had forty-two minutes to live.

He went home, took a shower, and then decided to drive rather than walk the four or maybe six blocks to Nicole's house (to return her mother's glasses that were left at the restaurant), so he could go on later to meet friends for drinks.

I believe that around 10:00 PM O.J. called Nicole, saying he wanted to drop something off for Sydney. It was a ruse. Nicole didn't want to see him, though, and so I believe she told him two fatal lies: that the kids weren't there, they were with her parents, and that somebody was coming over.

These two statements, on top of her rejection of him, would have sent him into a rage: *Who the fuck does she think she is? Who is she going to see? Why aren't the kids there? Why is she abandoning my kids to fuck around?*

O.J. left Rockingham and drove to Bundy. He checked the front of her residence to see if there were any cars there that he recognized. Seeing none, he pulled up behind the Bundy residence.

Nicole was upstairs playing soft music, drawing a bath. She was tense and needed to relax. The kids were sleeping. She lit candles around the bathtub. She picked up a cup of Ben and Jerry's ice cream and walked downstairs with it, wondering if Goldman had dropped the glasses outside the door.

I do believe it was likely that Nicole and Ron had been intimate before, but I don't believe that anything had been planned on the night of their deaths. The bath and the candles and the music were to help her relax, not for him. The kids were upstairs and she was not in the mood for romance. In fact, O.J.'s call made her a little more tense, a little more nervous. On her way to the door, she thinks she hears something. Deep down, she knows O.J. is there, in her bushes, spying on her. She can feel it. She pulls open her knife drawer and takes a knife with her, just in case.*

O.J., looking through her window, sees the candles and hears the soft music playing. He sees her coming to the door. He ducks into the shrubs, but when she opens the door, the light from inside the house pours out and exposes O.J. They're both startled, and then they start yelling at each other:

Who are the fucking candles for? How about the music? Who the fuck is that for? None of your business. Leave me alone. I'm calling 911.

She turns to go inside and call 911. O.J., furious that she's turned her back on him, punches the back of her head. She wasn't very tall. He hits her again. *Fucking bitch.* After she hits the ground, he sees that she had a knife.* *Fucking bitch pull a fucking knife on me.* Nicole is now lying on the ground. He hears somebody coming up the sidewalk, and hides. Ron Goldman comes walking up the walkway. He sees Nicole and rushes to her side. People think that O.J. attacked Goldman. I believe that it was the other way around. Nicole had told Goldman about O.J.'s propensity for violence, and when he sees O.J. in the bushes he goes after him.

---

*This is, if we are to believe O.J.'s statement to me that he didn't bring the knife. But like everything else, O.J. always wanted deniability. It is widely believed that O.J. brought a lock-back Swiss Army knife. He was never able to explain away the empty knife box that Mark Fuhrman found at Rockingham.

At first Goldman has the upper hand, but O.J. has the knife.

Goldman receives four fatal wounds—two in his chest, one in his abdomen, and one in his throat. With every beat of his heart, he loses massive amounts of blood . . . he is dying.

As Goldman is dying, Nicole starts to regain consciousness. She tries to get to the sidewalk to run away, to scream for help. She has just reached the steps when O.J. regains control of her. He stabs her twice in the neck in his effort to halt her progress to the street. Then O.J. pushes her to the ground, pulls her head up by the hair, and cuts her throat. The cut is so powerful it slices through her every artery, her trachea, everything, all the way to her spine, actually nicking the bone.

O.J. drops her into her own blood, where she crumples; dead by the time she hits the ground. O.J. quickly regains some of his composure, standing over Nicole, looking at her, knowing that she is dead. He starts walking down the sidewalk to the back of the condo, looking back over his shoulder. For a moment, he thinks Goldman might still be alive. O.J. walks back over to Goldman to check. This also explains why the bloody shoeprints went away from the crime scene and then back up the walkway. Goldman is dead.

O.J. goes back to his car, dripping blood, and sees that his middle finger had been cut badly. (In the Bronco, the police found a mixture of Ron's, Nicole's, and O.J.'s blood.)

He pulls out of the driveway, gets to the intersection of San Vicente, almost hits a woman in the intersection—Jill Shively—and yells at her: *Get the fuck out of the way.* Alarmed and angered, she takes down his license plate. (Marcia Clark never used Shively as a witness, and was, according to Shively, very hostile to her. She discounted Shively's credibility as a witness, because an ex-boyfriend ran a smear campaign against her and because she sold her story to a tabloid for $5,000. That was Marcia's first big mistake. This woman *saw O.J. leaving the scene of the crime* and even wrote down his license plate number accurately.)

O.J. drives home in a panic. He knows he has to make his flight, get the hell out of Dodge. As he pulls up to park, he sees the limo waiting for him and he knows he can't let the driver, Allan Park, see him. His alibi has to be that he was at home all night. (He testified that he alternately napped and chipped golf balls, at 10:00 PM, before catching a red-eye to Chicago, which has to be the lamest alibi I have ever heard in my life. O.J. would never have taken a nap before a night flight to Chicago, and he would never have chipped golf balls in the dark. To my knowledge, they never found any golf balls either.)

Not seeing the Bronco in the driveway, Allan Park had called the house and received no answer. But of course O.J. didn't know that.

When O.J. pulls in front of the Ashford gate and sees the limo, he backs up the Bronco onto Rockingham and parks it askew. To avoid the limo driver, he walks along the fence line between his house and the house next door, and then, out of the line of sight of the driver, he jumps over the fence, but he loses his balance and drops the glove from his pocket. He falls on the landing, hitting the wall—a thump that Kato Kaelin heard. O.J. goes through the kitchen entrance to the house.

He goes upstairs, grabs a towel, and wraps it around his hand. He ransacks his cabinet looking for bandages. He changes out of his clothes. They aren't very bloody because most of Goldman's blood soaked into his own clothing, and there was not much blood pressure left when the final wound was inflicted. Nicole's blood and some of her hair was found on the glove—from O.J. pulling her head back as he cut her throat. And as he was standing above and *behind* her when he murdered her, the blood poured away from him. Unfortunately for O.J., some of Nicole's and Ron's blood had splashed on his dark socks, which he didn't realize. He pulls his shirt off, reaches into his closet, gets a small black bag, puts every-thing he has from the crime scene, the shirt, the pants, the knife, the shoes—everything goes into the black bag (except for the socks). Then he realizes…*where are the gloves and the cap?* He goes back downstairs. His bandage, soaked through, drips blood from the foyer all the way to his Bronco. He can't find the gloves or the knit cap. He also knows that the most important thing now is to get away from the house, away from the crime scene. He goes back in the house. Kato stops him, worried about the thumps he heard in the back yard. O.J. looks around for a minute, then says, "Don't worry about it, it was nothing."

He and Kato and the driver start putting his luggage in the limo. He tells the driver he overslept. He won't let either of them touch the black bag. "I'll take that one with me," he says, and later Park testified that O.J. was rummaging through his "bags" in the car en route to the airport. He was probably still hoping to find the missing gloves and cap in there. As they drive to the airport, he is sweating immensely, opening the windows. They get to the airport. As Allan Park is getting O.J.'s luggage out, he looks over and notices that O.J. is standing by the trash can. I believe that at that moment O.J. was throwing the black bag with all the evidence into the garbage, covering it with other trash. Think about it. It was the perfect moment, the limo driver wasn't looking, nobody would notice. He sure wasn't going to bring it on the plane with him, because by the time he landed, the cops would have found the bodies. So O.J. walks over, gives a glance, drops his bag in, covers it with papers, and hopes against hope that the trash is emptied before the bodies are found, which is exactly what happened. The trash at LAX is picked up every couple of hours, it turns out. He gets on the flight. He starts concocting his alibi. *Okay, I'm just going to say that I overslept.* That whole story about where he got the cut on his knuckle in the hotel room in Chicago is total bullshit. It fell apart miserably when he was questioned by the police detectives Phillip Vannatter and Tom Lange (I feel they were pretty incompetent though, and instead of arresting him then and there, they simply let him go).

If there had been a less rigorous garbage disposal schedule at LAX, this trial would have been much shorter, and O.J. would have been in prison for the rest of his life. The truth was in that black bag. The black bag went to one of the biggest garbage dumps in any city in the world.

Somewhere in a landfill are the fossils of this crime, the decayed evidence, the knife, probably rusty and probably still with dried blood on it, and the Bruno Magli shoes.

I bet O.J. offers a special prayer of thanks to the garbage collectors of L.A. County. He always did appreciate people who did their jobs, and did them well.

TIMELINE OF THE NICOLE BROWN SIMPSON AND RON GOLDMAN MURDERS, JUNE 12, 1994

Sunday June 12, 1994, was a mild day, weather-wise, in Los Angeles. O.J. Simpson had spent the morning playing golf, and then later, cards in the clubhouse. Nicole Brown Simpson spent the morning shopping and getting ready for her daughter Sydney's dance recital. Mike Gilbert was climbing with his son David in Yosemite National Park. Marcus Allen was preparing for a trip to the Cayman Islands with his wife, Kathryn. Ron Goldman had spent the morning playing softball and was going to work at Mezzaluna restaurant later that evening. In other words, it began as a typical Sunday morning, but ended in tragedy. The details of the rest of the day are much more concrete as they involve a bloody double homicide that saw a sports hero and legend arrested.

2 PM	Brian "Kato" Kaelin, a friend and houseguest, sees O.J. in the kitchen of his Rockingham mansion. O.J. makes a series of calls to women. He first calls his then girlfriend Paula Barbieri. They argue about her desire to attend his daughter Sydney's recital. Paula instead flies to Las Vegas and spends the evening with singer Michael Bolton. In a

conversation with Traci Adell, O.J. says he's unhappy. He then calls Jasmine Guy, an actress.

4:00   Simpson asks Kaelin to set up a date for him on Tuesday and then leaves for Sydney's recital.

4:30   Nicole and her family arrive at Paul Revere Middle School for Sydney's recital. Goldman arrives for work at Mezzaluna restaurant.

4:45   O.J. arrives for the recital. He sits behind Nicole and her family. He would later move to a corner to talk with his friend Ron Fischman.

6:15   After the recital, O.J. carries on a pleasant conversation with the Browns.

6:30–7:00   Nicole and her guests arrive at Mezzaluna. At Rockingham, O.J. tells Kaelin he's unhappy that Nicole was wearing a tight dress and did not allow him to go to the restaurant.

7:35   O.J. calls former Los Angeles Raiderette Gretchen Stockdale and leaves a message: "It's Orenthal Jones, [sic] who is finally at a place in his life where he is, like, totally, totally unattached."

8:30   Nicole and her family leave Mezzaluna.

9:00   Faye Resnick calls Nicole from rehab. She claims that Nicole says she told Simpson: "Get away from us! Get out of my life. You're not welcome with this family anymore."

9:03   Kaelin calls his friend Tom O'Brien, but O.J. interrupts him and asks for twenty dollars for dinner.

9:10   O.J. and Kaelin take Simpson's Bentley to McDonald's.

9:25   O.J. eats on the way home after Kaelin had paid for both meals.

9:33   Goldman ends work shift.

9:35   Kaelin leaves O.J. at the estate near his Bentley.

9:37   Juditha Brown, Nicole's mother, calls Mezzaluna and reports that she has left her glasses.

9:40   Juditha Brown calls Nicole concerning her glasses.

9:45   Nicole calls Mezzaluna and talks to Karen Lee Crawford and Goldman. Goldman takes the glasses to his home and changes before driving to Nicole's condo.

9:45 or 9:50 Rosa Lopez, a maid at Simpson's neighbor's house, hears O.J.'s dog barking.

10:10	Kaelin calls his friend Rachel Ferrara from the guest house.
10:15	Nicole's neighbors say they heard a dog barking. Prosecutors say that this is the time of the murders.
10:22	Limousine driver Allan Park arrives at Rockingham to take O.J. to the airport for a flight to Chicago. Park stops on a side street to wait for O.J.
10:30	One of Nicole's neighbors, Steven Schwab, takes his dog for a walk.
10:40	Park walks up to Rockingham and rings the bell several times, but he receives no answer. At the same time, a resident near Nicole's house reports hearing someone yell "Hey" three times.
10:40–10:45	Kaelin, who is still on the phone with Ferrara, says he heard thumps on his wall near the air conditioner.
10:43	Park tries to page his boss, Dale St. John.
10:49	Park calls St. John to say no one is answering at the estate.
10:55	Park sees Kaelin near the house, as a tall African American figure approaches the front door.
10:56	Kaelin lets Park into the house. Schwab finds Nicole's dog.
11:01–11:02	O.J. comes out of the house to pack up the limo. He and Kaelin briefly search for an intruder who could have been responsible for the thumping sound.
11:05	Schwab returns home with Nicole's dog.
11:10–11:15	Park and O.J. leave for the airport.
11:40	Sukru Boztepe, Schwab's neighbor, takes Nicole's dog and sees red spots on its legs and paws.
11:45	O.J. leaves for Chicago on American Airlines Flight 668.
Midnight	Boztepe and his wife, Bettina Rasmussen, take Nicole's dog for a walk. He takes them back to Nicole's condo.
12 AM	Boztepe and his wife discover the bodies of Ron Goldman and Nicole Brown Simpson. Boztepe and his wife were still visibly shaken by the incident even during their testimonies during the trial.
12:13	Officers Riski and Terrazas arrive at the crime scene.
2:10	Detective Mark Fuhrman arrives at Bundy.
4:05	Tom Lange arrives at the crime scene.
4:25	Phil Vannatter arrives at the crime scene.

THE SIMPSON TRIAL TIMELINE

June 1994

June 13: Noon—O.J. returns to Los Angeles. After being put in handcuffs he is taken to police headquarters for three hours of questioning.

June 15: Robert Shapiro takes over O.J.'s defense.

June 16: O.J. and his children Sydney and Justin, along with hundreds of friends and family, attend Nicole's funeral.

June 17: O.J. charged with two counts of murder with special circumstances. Simpson does not surrender to the police, but rather leads them on 60-mile low-speed car chase across freeways from Orange County to Rockingham. 9:00 PM: O.J. is finally arrested and jailed without bail.

July 1994

July 8: Municipal Judge Kathleen Kennedy-Powell says there is enough evidence to put O.J. on trial after six days of preliminary hearings.

July 20:	O.J. offers $500,000 reward for information that would lead to the arrest of the "real killer or killers." Shapiro sets up a national toll-free hotline for tips.
July 22:	O.J. pleads "absolutely, 100% not guilty." Simpson's case is assigned to Superior Court Judge Lance Ito.
July 27:	Ron Goldman's birth mother files a wrongful death suit against O.J., saying that he "willfully, wantonly, and maliciously" murdered her son.
July 30:	Grand jury transcripts describe a jealous O.J. who stalked Nicole.

August 1994

| Aug. 22: | Court papers show that some DNA tests match the genetic makeup of O.J.'s blood with that of samples from the blood trail leading from murder scene. |

September 1994

| Sept. 9: | Prosecutors say they will pursue a life sentence without the option of parole for O.J. if he is convicted. |
| Sept. 26: | Jury selection begins. |

November 1994

| Nov. 3: | Jury of eight women and four men is selected. Panel includes eight blacks, one white, one Hispanic, and two people of mixed race. |

December 1994

| Dec. 8: | An alternate jury is selected. It consists of nine women and three men, including seven blacks, four whites, and one Hispanic. |

January 1995

Jan. 4:   Defense abandons challenge of DNA evidence.

Jan. 8:   Word leaks out that O.J. is planning to write a book
                     titled *I Want to Tell You* as a response to 300,000 letters
                     that he received in jail.

Jan. 11:   The jury is sequestered in a secret location, while pros-
                     ecutors release documents accusing O.J. of a history of
                     abuse against Nicole.

Jan. 12:   Ito hears defense arguments that question the racial
                     attitudes of Detective Mark Fuhrman, who discovered
                     the bloody glove at Rockingham.

Jan. 23:   Opening statements by prosecution and defense. Ito
                     dismisses two jurors.

Jan. 31:   The first witness for the prosecution is Sharyn Gilbert,
                     the 911 operator who answered a call from O.J.'s home
                     at 3:58 AM on Jan. 1, 1989. She said she heard a woman
                     screaming and "someone being hit." John Edwards, the
                     officer who came to the scene in 1989, describes the
                     event in his testimony. "Then a woman came running
                     out of the bushes to my left, across the driveway. She
                     was a female Caucasian, blond hair. She was wearing a
                     bra only as an upper garment and she had on dark—I
                     believe it was a dark, lightweight sweatpants or night
                     pajama bottom and she ran across and collapsed on the
                     speaker—the identical kind of a speaker post on the
                     inside of the gate. She collapsed on it and started yelling,
                     'He's going to kill me, he's going to kill me.' Then she
                     pressed the button which allowed the gate to open and
                     she ran out again, yelling, 'He's going to kill me.'"

February 1995

Feb. 1–2:   O.J.'s friend Ronald Shipp testifies that O.J. told him
                     that he dreamed of killing Nicole one night after the
                     murders.

Feb. 3, 6:   Nicole's sister Denise Brown testifies that O.J. was abu-
                     sive toward her sister.

Feb. 7:	Nicole's neighbor Pablo Fenjves says he heard a dog's "plaintive wail" from near her condo at 10:15 PM. This is the first move toward establishing the time of the murders.
Feb. 12:	Jurors tour crime scene and Rockingham. They also see Mezzaluna and Ron Goldman's apartment.
Feb. 27:	Rosa Lopez, Simpson's neighbor's maid, testifies out of turn and on videotape that she saw O.J.'s Bronco outside his estate at 10:15 PM.

March 1995

March 9–10, 13–16:	Detective Mark Fuhrman describes finding the glove at Rockingham and declares he had not uttered a racial slur in ten years.
March 22–23, 27–28:	Brian "Kato" Kaelin says he last saw O.J. at 9:35 PM on night of killings. He testified that Simpson was "upset" after an earlier altercation with Nicole. Later in the trial, during the prosecution's questioning, he said under oath that he wouldn't lie for O.J.
March 28:	Limo driver Allan Park says that O.J. didn't answer the doorbell at his home from 10:40 PM until about 11:00 PM.

April 1995

| April 6–7: | Juror illness closes court. Dismissed juror Jeanette Harris says that there are racial divisions within the jury. |
| April 21: | The jury strikes over the dismissal of three deputies who had accompanied them. |

May 1995

| May 8–12, 15: | DNA lab director Robin Cotton gives astronomical odds from blood examinations that incriminate Simpson. |

June 1995

June 2, 6–9, 12–15:   Coroner shows jurors graphic pictures of Ron and Nicole and explains in depth how they were murdered. In his report, the coroner says of Nicole's wound, "The incised wound of the neck is gaping and exposes the larynx and cervical vertebral column."

June 15:   O.J. tries on leather gloves linked to the murders. He can barely squeeze his hands in. He tells jury, "They don't fit."

July 1995

July 7:   After the prosecution rests, Judge Ito denies the defense's request for an immediate innocent verdict due to a lack of sufficient evidence.

July 10:   Arnelle Simpson, O.J.'s oldest daughter, testifies as first defense witness. She attacks Ronald Shipp's testimony about O.J.'s dream of killing Nicole.

July 11:   Danny Mandel testifies that he and his date walked past Nicole's condo at 10:20 PM. He said he didn't see anything unusual. This raises doubts concerning the prosecution's estimate of time of murder. Robert Heidstra says he was walking his dogs at 10:35 PM, and heard men arguing near Nicole's condo, suggesting a new time of killings.

July 14, 17–18:   Robert Huzienga, O.J.'s doctor, agrees with the defense's contention that O.J. had debilitating injuries from his football career. However, he says that O.J. was physically capable of carrying out the murders.

July 24:   Frederic Rieders, a forensic toxicologist, says he found evidence of blood preservative in two pieces of evidence. This implies that the blood was planted by police.

July 28:   A North Carolina judge blocks the defense's attempts to force a screenwriter to hand over taped interviews of Detective Fuhrman. The defense says the tapes show Fuhrman using a racial slur which he had repeatedly denied using.

August 1995

Aug. 2: Microbiologist John Gerdes says that the L.A. police crime lab is "by far" the most contaminated he's ever seen. His testimony raises uncertainty about the most widely used DNA test.

Aug. 7: A North Carolina appeals court allows the defense to acquire tapes of Fuhrman using racial epithet.

Aug. 9: Ito ends the defense's efforts to question two reporters about DNA evidence leaks.

Aug. 10–11: Michael Baden, ex-New York City medical examiner, raises doubts about the prosecution's theory on how the murders happened.

Aug. 15: The prosecution calls on Ito to step down after his wife, police captain Margaret York, is derided by Fuhrman in tapes. Another judge steps in to make the decision.

Aug. 17: Gilbert Aguilar, a police fingerprint specialist, says that O.J.'s prints were not among the seventeen sets at crime scene. Fuhrman, however, noted that there were two fingerprints on the gate to the property. They had been subsequently smudged, however.

Aug. 18: Ito stays on the case after another judge blocks York's testimony about Fuhrman.

Aug. 22–25, 28: Forensics expert Henry Lee says he found that the three shoeprints at the crime scene didn't match O.J.'s Bruno Magli shoes. He claims that police mishandled the evidence.

Aug. 29: Excerpts of recorded interviews between Fuhrman and screenwriter Laura Hart McKinny were played with the jury absent. Fuhrman calmly used the word "nigger" forty-one times and gave accounts of police brutality.

Aug. 31:   Ito rules defense can tell jury of two instances of Fuhrman using the slur, but cannot use the described misconduct.

September 1995

Sept. 5:   Five witnesses, including McKinny, testify that Fuhrman used the racial slur within the last ten years. At a hearing with the jury not present, Fuhrman invokes Fifth Amendment protection in further testimony.

Sept. 7:   Ito announces that he will give the jury vague reasons about why Fuhrman will not testify. The prosecution appeals this decision.

Sept. 8:   Appeals court rules Ito cannot even give a vague hint about Fuhrman invoking the Fifth Amendment.

Sept. 11:   The defense refuses to rest while the appeals court rules on Furhman. Ito orders the prosecution to begin their rebuttal. Five photographers testify about pictures of O.J. wearing gloves like ones linked to crime.

Sept. 12:   Glove expert says he's "100 percent certain" gloves were the same.

Sept. 13:   State crime lab expert says the most sophisticated DNA test finds Goldman's blood in Simpson's Bronco.

Sept. 14:   Prosecution forensics expert Douglas Deedrick contradicts the defense's contention that there was a second set of shoe prints at the murder scene.

Sept. 18:   The prosecution tentatively closes its rebuttal but retains the right to call more witnesses to rebut new defense testimony, which it uses later.

Sept. 19:   Defense puts former mobster Craig Anthony Fiato on the stand to testify that L.A. detective Philip Vannatter is a liar. Simpson applies to register his name as an exclusive trademark. The move was instigated by Mike Gilbert upon seeing all the O.J. merchandise being produced. Gilbert wanted to protect O.J.'s name from being used distastefully on merchandise.

Sept. 20: Ito reprimands both the prosecution and the defense: "It's astonishing what we've sunk to," as arguing over minor issues persists.

Sept. 21: Ito announces his jury instructions will include the possibility of finding Simpson guilty of second-degree murder. This is a huge setback for the defense.

Sept. 22: Simpson is allowed to address the jury without being cross-examined. He says he "did not, would not, could not have committed this crime."

Sept. 26: Clark begins her closing arguments by admonishing her former star witness—Mark Fuhrman—as a racist. She does, however, warn that that fact does not mean that he planted evidence at Simpson's home. [This turned out to be a huge mistake for Clark. She vilified her star witness in the eyes of the jury. She asked, and answered her own question, "Should the LAPD ever have hired him? No. Should such a person be a police officer? No."]

Sept. 27: Christopher Darden ends the prosecution's closing arguments by portraying Simpson as consumed by a jealous rage. Cochran then takes up for the defense, hammering home the theme "If it doesn't fit, you must acquit."

Sept. 28: Cochran calls upon history and the Bible and ends by telling jurors "God bless you." Barry Scheck says jurors cannot trust any of the DNA analysis on blood because of police contamination and tampering.

Sept. 29: There are more than sixty objections from defense lawyers. Darden and Clark finish their prosecution rebuttal with a video display portraying everything from Nicole's 1989 911 call to photos of the bloody victims. At 4:08 PM Ito turns the case over to the jury, reminding them to ignore warnings from both sides that "the world is watching."

October 1995

Oct. 2:   The jury begins deliberations shortly after 9:00 AM.
                                They break to hear the testimony of the limousine dri-
                                ver who picked Simpson up on the night of the mur-
                                ders, and return a verdict.

Oct. 3:   Verdict of not guilty is announced and O.J. Simpson is
                                set free.

MEMO BY DETECTIVE MARK FUHRMAN ON 1985 DOMESTIC DISPUTE AT SIMPSON'S HOME

A memo Detective Mark Fuhrman wrote on January 18, 1989, regarding a 1985 domestic dispute at Simpson's estate. Fuhrman said he wrote it at the request of a detective and the city attorney's office. There are reports that Nicole called the police twelve times over the course of their relationship.

During the fall or winter of 1985 I responded to a 415 family dispute at 360 N. Rockingham. Upon arrival I observed two persons in the front of the estate, a male black pacing on the driveway and a female wht sitting on a veh crying. I inquired if the persons I observed were the residents at which time the male black stated, "Yeah, I own this, I'm O.J. Simpson!" My attention turned to the female who was sobbing and asked her if she was alright but before she could speak the male black (Simpson) interrupted stating, "she's my wife, she's okay!" During my conversation with the female I noted that she was sitting in front of a shattered windshield (Mercedes-Benz I believe) and I asked, "who broke the windshield?" with the female responding, "he did (pointing to Simpson).... He hit the windshield with a baseball bat!" Upon hearing the female's statement Simpson exclaimed, "I broke the windshield ... it's mine ... there's no trouble here." I turned to the female and asked if she would like to make a report and she stated, "no."

It seems odd to remember such an event but it is not everyday that you respond to a celebrity's home for a family dispute. For this reason this incident was indelibly pressed in my memory.

From trial transcripts at http://walraven.org/simpson/fuhr-rpt.html.

APPENDIX V

NICOLE BROWN SIMPSON'S UNDATED LETTER TO O.J.*

These are excerpts from the letter that was introduced in the civil trial. The text was taken (spelling errors included) from a handwritten letter.

O.J.—

I think I have to put this all in a letter. Alot of years ago I used to do much better in a letter, I'm gonna try it again now.

I'd like you to keep this letter if we split, so that you'll always know why we split. I'd also like you to keep it if we stay together, as a reminder.

Right now I am so angry! If I didn't know that the courts would take Sydney & Justin away from me if I did this I would (expletive) every guy including some that you know just to let you know how it feels.

I wish someone could explain all this to me. I see our marriage as a huge mistake & you don't.

---

*This was taken from the trial transcripts at http://walraven.org/simpson/nb-to-oj.html.

I knew what went on in our relationship before we got married. I knew after 6 years that all the things I thought were going on—were! All the things I gave in to—all the "I'm sorry for thinking that" "I'm sorry for not believing you"—"I'm sorry for not trusting you."

I made up with you all the time & even took the blame many times for your cheating. I know this took place because we fought about it alot & even discussed it before we got married with my family & a minister.

OK before the marriage I lived with it & dealt with (illegible) mainly because you finally said that we weren't married at the time.

I assumed that your recurring nasty attitude & mean streak was to cover up your cheating & a general disrespect for women & a lack of manners!...

I let my guard down—I thought it was finally gonna be you & me—you wanted a baby (so you said) & I wanted a baby—then with each pound you were terrible. You gave me dirty looks looks of disgust—said mean things to me at times about my appearance walked out on me & lied to me....

There was also that time before Justin & after few months Sydney, I felt really good about how I got back into shape and we made out. You beat the holy hell out of me & we lied at the X-ray lab & said I fell off a bike...Remember!??

Great for my self esteem....

And since Justin birth & the mad New Years Eve beat up.

I just don't see how our stories compare—I was so bad because I wore sweats & left shoes around & didn't keep a perfect house or comb my hair the way you liked it—or had dinner ready at the precise moment you walked through the door or that I just plain got on your nerves sometimes.

I just don't see how that compares to infidelity, wife beating verbal abuse—

I just don't think everybody goes through this—

And if I wanted to hurt you or had it in me to be anything like the person you are—I would have done so after the (illegible) incident. But I didn't even do it then. I called the cops to save my life whether you believe it or not. But I didn't pursue anything after that—I didn't prosecute, I didn't call the press & I didn't make a big charade out of it. I waited for it to die down and asked for it to. But I've never loved you since or been the same.

It made me take a look at my life with you—my wonderful life with the superstar that wonderful man, O.J. Simpson the father of my kids—that husband of that terribly insecure (illegible)—the girl with no self esteem (illegible) of worth— she must be (illegible) those things to with a guy like that.

It certainly doesn't take a strong person to be with a guy like that and certainly no one would be envious of that life. . . .

I just believe that a relationship is based on trust—and the last time I trusted you was at our wedding ceremony. it's just so hard for me to trust you again. Even though you say you're a different guy. That O.J. Simpson guy brought me alot of pain heatache—I tried so hard with him—I wanted so to be a good wife. But he never gave me a chance.

The National Domestic Violence Hotline

Phone: 1.800.799.SAFE (7233)   TTY: 1.800.787.3224   www.ndvh.org

Hotline advocates provide support and assistance to anyone involved in a domestic violence situation. All calls to the National Domestic Violence Hotline are confidential.

APPENDIX VI

O.J.'S SUICIDE LETTER*

This letter was read by Bob Kardashian on the radio on the day of the slow-speed Bronco chase. It has been edited for spelling.

To whom it may concern:

First, everyone understand I have nothing to do with Nicole's murder. I loved her, always have and always will. If we had a problem, it's because I loved her so much.

Recently, we came to the understanding that for now we were not right for each other, at least for now. Despite our love we were different, and that's why we mutually agreed to go our separate ways.

It was tough splitting for a second time, but we both knew it was for the best. Inside I had no doubt that in the future, we would be close as friends or more. Unlike what

---

has been written in the press, Nicole and I had a great relationship for most of our lives together.

Like all long-term relationships, we had a few downs and ups. I took the heat New Year's 1989 because that's what I was supposed to do. I did not plead no contest for any other reason but to protect our privacy and was advised it would end the press hype.

I don't want to belabor knocking the press, but I can't believe what is being said. Most of it is totally made up. I know you have a job to do, but as a last wish, please, please, please, leave my children in peace. Their lives will be tough enough.

I want to send my love and thanks to all my friends. I'm sorry I can't name every one of you, especially A.C. man, thanks for being in my life. The support and friendship I received from so many: Wayne Hughes, Lewis Markes, Frank Olson, Mark Packer, Bender, Bobby Kardashian. I wish we had spent more time together in recent years.

My golfing buddies, Hoss, Alan Austin, Mike, Craig, Bender, Wyler, Sandy, Jay, Donnie, thanks for the fun.

All my teammates over the years, Reggie, you were the soul of my pro career. Ahmad, I never stopped being proud of you. Marcus, You've got a great lady in Catherine, don't mess it up. Bobby Chandler, thanks for always being there. Skip and Kathy, I love you guys, without you I never would have made it through this far. Marguerite, thanks for the early years. We had some fun.

Paula, what can I say? You are special. I'm sorry we're not going to have our chance. God brought you to me I now see. As I leave, you'll be in my thoughts. I think of my life and feel I've done most of the right things.

What the outcome, people will look and point. I can't take that. I can't subject my children to that. This way they can move on and go on with their lives. Please, if I've done anything worthwhile in my life. Let my kids live in peace from you (press).

I've had a good life. I'm proud of how I lived. My mama taught me to do un to other. I treated people the way I wanted to be treated. I've always tried to be up and helpful so why is this happening?

I'm sorry for the Goldman family. I know how much it hurts. Nicole and I had a good life together. All this press talk about a rocky relationship was no more than what every long-term relationship experiences. All her friends will confirm that I have been totally loving and under-standing of what she's been going through.

At times I have felt like a battered husband or boyfriend but I loved her, make that clear to everyone. And I would take whatever it took to make it work.

Don't feel sorry for me. I've had a great life, great friends. Please think of the real O.J. and not this lost person. Thanks for making my life special. I hope I helped yours.

Peace and love, O.J.

PEOPLE AND PLACES GLOSSARY

People

Marcus Allen: Professional football player and close friend of O.J., whom he considered a mentor. He is believed by O.J.'s inner circle, however, to have been involved in a budding romantic relationship with Nicole Brown Simpson at the time of her murder.

F. Lee Bailey: Part of O.J.'s Dream Team of lawyers during his criminal trial.

Paula Barbieri: O.J.'s girlfriend at the time of the murders.

Al Beardsley: Involved in the Las Vegas hotel room raid, he told Thomas Riccio, who then told O.J., that there were memorabilia that belonged to O.J. in the Vegas hotel room.

Lou Brown: Father of Nicole Brown Simpson.

Tammy Bruce: Former head of NOW in Los Angeles. She was viciously opposed to O.J. and sparked a flood of threats against his life and those close to him after his acquittal.

Marcia Clark: One of the central members of the prosecution team against O.J.

Johnnie Cochran: One of O.J.'s main lawyers. He coined the now famous catch-phrase, "If it doesn't fit, you must acquit." This was in reference to the murderer's glove that didn't fit O.J.'s hand in the courtroom.

Al Cowlings: Known as A.C., he was O.J.'s best friend. They played football together from high school, through college, and into the pros. A.C. was driving the white Bronco during the infamous low-speed car chase.

Chris Darden: One of the central members of the prosecution team against O.J.

Bruce Fromong: The sports memorabilia collector and salesman who was O.J.'s target in the Las Vegas hotel room raid in 2007.

Mark Fuhrman: The LAPD detective who found the bloody glove at the crime scene. He was later accused of racist remarks and the defense for O.J. Simpson used that to discredit his testimony.

Fred Goldman: Ron Goldman's father. He has been diligent in his attempts to collect compensation from O.J. after a civil suit that concluded that O.J. was responsible for the murders of Ron Goldman and Nicole Brown Simpson.

Kim Goldman: Sister of Ron Goldman.

Ron Goldman: Friend of Nicole Brown Simpson's. He had come to Nicole's house to return her mother's glasses that she left at the Mezzaluna restaurant. He was murdered that night along with Nicole.

Brian "Kato" Kaelin: A house guest at Rockingham and aspiring actor at the time of O.J.'s arrest and trial. He testified concerning O.J.'s mood and whereabouts around the time of the murders.

Bob Kardashian: Friend of O.J.'s. On the day of the low-speed car chase, he read Simpson's apparent suicide note on the radio. He later "sold out" O.J. in a book deal with Larry Schiller. He also carried O.J.'s Louis Vuitton bag into Rockingham, which many wrongly suspected held O.J.'s bloody clothes.

Tom Lange: One of the detectives, along with Phil Vannatter, who led the initial questioning of O.J. after the murders.

Dan Leonard: One of O.J.'s lawyers in the civil trial of 1996. He deposed Marcus Allen about his involvement with Nicole.

Christy Lutkemeier: Friend of Mike Gilbert who alerted him that much of his O.J. Simpson memorabilia had been removed from a storage unit by Bruce Fromong, which he took to his house and later to a Las Vegas hotel room.

Christie Prody: O.J.'s young girlfriend in Florida. They have had a tumultuous relationship involving abuse and pandering to the tabloids. Since 2000, the police have been called to their house five times.

Nicole Pulvers: An attorney assigned to stay with O.J. while he was in prison during his trial. Initially, he could have visitors only if she were present.

Cathy Randa: O.J.'s personal assistant. She, like most of the people close to O.J., did not approve of his attempts to get back together with Nicole after their divorce.

Judith Regan: The publisher who brokered the deal for O.J.'s "hypothetical" tell-all book, *If I Did It*.

Faye Resnick: A new and close friend of Nicole Brown Simpson. She advised Nicole to distance herself from O.J. and is a main source of information concerning Nicole's confrontations with O.J. and her budding affair with Marcus Allen. O.J. consistently blames Faye for Nicole's death.

Thomas Riccio: He told O.J. about the location of the memorabilia, and also brought a tape recorder to the room and sold the recording to TMZ.com immediately after the incident.

Sharon Rufo: Ron Goldman's mother and Fred Goldman's ex-wife.

Larry Schiller: Photojournalist, author, and movie producer/ director who published *American Tragedy: The Inside Story of the Simpson Defense* in collaboration with Bob Kardashian.

Robert Shapiro: Part of O.J.'s Dream Team of lawyers during his criminal trial.

Ron Shipp: A close friend of O.J.'s who eventually testified against O.J. for the prosecution.

Arnelle Simpson: Daughter of O.J. and his previous wife, Marguerite.

Eunice Simpson: O.J.'s mother.

Jason Simpson: Son of O.J. and his previous wife, Marguerite.

Justin Simpson: Son of O.J. and Nicole Simpson.

Marguerite Simpson: First wife of O.J. Simpson and mother of his daughter Arnelle and son Jason. She was also the mother of his daughter Aaren, who drowned at age two.

Nicole Brown Simpson: Second and ex-wife of O.J. Simpson. She was murdered along with Ron Goldman on June 12, 1994.

O.J. Simpson: Former college and professional football star and member of the NFL Hall of Fame. Accused, and later acquitted, of killing his ex-wife Nicole Brown and her friend Ron Goldman. He will stand trial in September 2008 for several charges, including armed robbery, conspiracy, and kidnapping.

Sydney Simpson: Daughter of O.J. and Nicole. She dialed 911 in 2004 saying that her father didn't love her and mentioning "the abuse thing."

Gretchen Stockdale: She briefly dated O.J. around the time of the murders and after his acquittal.

Skip Taft: O.J. Simpson's longtime friend and lawyer. Among O.J.'s inner circle, he was regarded as the wisest and most respected of the group.

Phil Vannatter: One of the detectives, along with Tom Lange, who led the initial questioning of O.J. after the murders.

Places

Hanford: A city in California near Fresno and in between San Francisco and Los Angeles. Home of Mike Gilbert.

Rockingham: The name of O.J.'s estate, named after the street it's located on: 360 N. Rockingham Ave.

Brentwood: The neighborhood in Western Los Angeles where O.J.'s Rockingham estate is located.

Bundy: Refers to the Bundy Drive neighborhood of Brentwood and the location of Nicole Brown Simpson's condo where she and Ron Goldman were murdered.

Mezzaluna: The Italian restaurant in Brentwood where Nicole Brown Simpson and her family went the night of her murder after a recital at her daughter Sydney's school. O.J. was not invited. This is where Ron Goldman worked and where Nicole's mother left her glasses, prompting Goldman to come to her home and return them later that night.

INDEX